I'd Like You to Meet My Neighbor

David Freeland Case

Cover Art

Jesus Brings Healing to the World is a picture of Jesus suspended over a sphere, representing the earth. There are numerous references to Biblical themes and historical events. The painting is the work of an Azerbaijani Neighbor whose story is told in chapter 2.

First, Jesus is suspended over a "broken world" as seen in the top right quadrant–3 cracks that have been bandaged with 3 bandages. We discussed this and thought perhaps the damage was caused by the "world system that is opposed to God's Law, the Flesh, and the Devil." The 3 bandages she didn't know about, but the viewer can use his own imagination. We discussed one possible meaning: Faith, Hope and Love...or Father, Son and Holy Spirit.

Above Jesus is a beautiful view of a heavenly paradise and below Jesus is a horrible view of hell fire.

To the left of Jesus appears 3 cloudy pillars–perhaps a reference to the way Jehovah led the ancient Hebrews from their enslavement in Egypt to the Promise given to their father Abraham…and eventually to the Promised One who would save them from more than slavery to man, but from slavery to sin.

Below that, in the lower left corner is an open cave with women–a probable reference to the faithful women who followed Jesus and who cared for His body after His death.

Jesus is pierced with 7 wounds, not including the wounded heart. Could this be possibly that 7 is the number of "completeness or perfection" or the 7 last words He spoke from the cross? The wounded heart is the only wound that is not oozing blood. We think it is His divine heart, broken for the salvation of the world while the other wounds show His human suffering.

The cross, or X shape is actually a scroll, or the structure of a scroll. We understand this to be a reference to Jesus being the Word Written of God; and the picture of Him upon the Cross is Jesus, the Living Word of God, dying for mankind's redemption – both revelations of God's love for all.

Prints of this painting can be ordered directly from the artist by contacting her at ksarnesar@gmail.com or by contacting the author to get information on how to order your own print.

David Freeland Case – dcaseps84.11@gmail.com

Copyright © 2016 by David Freeland Case

I'd Like You to Meet My Neighbor
How Cross Cultural Relationships Can Change You...and the World, One Friend at a Time
by David Freeland Case

Printed in the United States of America.

ISBN 9781498459730

All rights reserved solely by the author. The author guarantees all contents are original and do not infringe upon the legal rights of any other person or work. No part of this book may be reproduced in any form without the permission of the author. The views expressed in this book are not necessarily those of the publisher.

Unless otherwise indicated, Scripture quotations taken from The Message (MSG). Copyright © 1993, 1994, 1995, 1996, 2000, 2001, 2002. Used by permission of NavPress Publishing Group. Used by permission. All rights reserved.

www.xulonpress.com

About the Author:

Reverend David Case is an Anglican Deacon who has spent the past 20 years crossing cultures in the Washington DC area. His desire is to demonstrate, through this collection of true stories of internationals he has met in the US, that meaningful and redemptive relationships are possible all around us. The world has come nearer to us as international students and scholars, working professionals, immigrants and refugees – all known and loved by God…and people we can extend the love and light of Jesus to….should we chose to cross the cultural divides. Jesus did this for us – let's follow His example and do this for His sake and for the blessing of our neighbors from abroad. In this way, we become "Glo-cal" Christians – those who reach out to newcomers locally, and in so doing, have a global impact on families and communities.

Rev. David F. Case, Fairfax VA
Feast of the Epiphany 2016

DEDICATION

Dedicated to my father, Glenn Lewis Case, 1934-2015

My father grew up on a dairy farm in the Catskill Mountains of Upstate New York. He planted a church, became a school teacher, served as a Christian school principal; and later in his life, he came to be known as the "pastor" of the local Wal-mart. He had a strong work ethic, but he had a stronger friendship ethic. Everyone he met found him to be kind, caring and engaging. As he got to know people, his greatest desire was to share how much God loved them.

Thanks, dad, for your example to me and your kindness to so many others along your life's journey. I, and the world, are richer for having had you.

Credits/Thanks

A worthwhile project is usually a collaboration of many who offer ideas, inspiration, assistance and encouragement along the way. Writing "Neighbors" is no exception. I would like to acknowledge some of the many who helped me start, continue and complete this labor of love.

Fara Cepak was the first one to encourage me to put stories to paper (or computer.) She and later, Linda Sellevaag spent many hours proofreading, making suggestions and constructive comments. My sister-in-law, Karen Case, and my son, Josiah and his wife, Christine, carefully read and reviewed the manuscript, making invaluable comments on how to "tell it better." My nephew, Ben, was able to lend skillful technical support toward the end of the project with formatting and set up. Thank you all.

I also want to thank my Xulon team that worked with me to bring this book from my heart to your home. Kenneth Clark, Jennifer Kasper, Ruthy Deal, Tynesha Evans, Christopher Gonzales, Jason Fletcher, & Bethany Emerson.

I would be woefully remiss if I didn't mention two special ladies in my life: first, my closest and best neighbor, my wife Cathy, who has shared her heart and home with so many for so many years. Second, Nancy Drew Richards, who went from "stranger" to "acquaintance" to "friend" to "family" thanks in large part to Chinese food and fried chicken. Food is just one of God's ways to get people together as neighbors.

Last of all, I want to thank the special international friends who have shared their lives with me and allowed me the privilege of telling their stories. Thank you so much for showing me how to be a friend to such amazing people from so many different places and cultures.

Jesus answers the question: Who is My Neighbor?
Luke 10:25-37 The Message (MSG)

²⁵ Just then a religion scholar stood up with a question to test Jesus. "Teacher, what do I need to do to get eternal life?"

²⁶ He answered, "What's written in God's Law? How do you interpret it?"

²⁷ He said, "That you love the Lord your God with all your passion and prayer and muscle and intelligence—and that you love your neighbor as well as you do yourself."

²⁸ "Good answer!" said Jesus. "Do it and you'll live."

²⁹ Looking for a loophole, he asked, "And just how would you define 'neighbor'?"

³⁰⁻³² Jesus answered by telling a story. "There was once a man traveling from Jerusalem to Jericho. On the way he was attacked by robbers. They took his clothes, beat him up, and went off leaving him half-dead. Luckily, a priest was on his way down the same road, but when he saw him he angled across to the other side. Then a Levite religious man showed up; he also avoided the injured man.

³³⁻³⁵ "A Samaritan traveling the road came on him. When he saw the man's condition, his heart went out to him. He gave him first aid, disinfecting and bandaging his wounds. Then he lifted him onto his donkey, led him to an inn, and made him comfortable. In the morning he took out two silver coins and gave them to the innkeeper, saying, 'Take good care of him. If it costs any more, put it on my bill—I'll pay you on my way back.'

³⁶ "What do you think? Which of the three became a neighbor to the man attacked by robbers?"

³⁷ "The one who treated him kindly," the religion scholar responded.

Jesus said, "Go and do the same."

TABLE OF CONTENTS

Preface by Rev. Steven Schlossberg xv
Introduction xix

Chapter 1   Mr. A, from Afghanistan 25
Chapter 2   Azerbaijani Women Build a New Future for Themselves – One Painting and One Page at a Time 33
Chapter 3   Meet BK from Nepal 39
Chapter 4   A Chinese Scholar with a Hungry Heart 43
Chapter 5   "Enough!" – that is what my name means . . 53
Chapter 6   Hamdiya- A Slave Made Free 57
Chapter 7   My Japanese Neighbors— The Toyota Travelers 63
Chapter 8   My Pakistani Neighbor, Walter and His Funny Hat 69
Chapter 9   "No" and "Yes": Japanese and Bolivian Style 77
Chapter 10 What is better than "Turkish Delight?" . . . . more Turkish "Delights" 85

Epilogue 93
Conclusion 107

Preface – by Fr. Steven Schlossberg, Rector of St. Johns Troy, New York

Former director of the The Lamb Center (a day time drop center for the city's homeless population), Fairfax City, Virginia.

Specialization is sometimes said to be the bane of our age. The phenomenon has infected almost every profession, including law, including retail, including repair shops. But we most often hear it complained of in medicine. General practitioners treat fewer ailments than before; it sometimes seems they spend more of their time and energy making referrals than healing infirmities. No doubt this sometimes serves us well; a cancer patient, for example, prizes the special expertise of an oncologist But even within the discipline of oncology there are specializations, for which we are thankful. Specialization is a good fruit, certainly the inevitable consequence, of growing knowledge.

But the inevitable consequence has had consequences. Not just people with unusually complex diagnoses but almost everyone who is hospitalized for anything finds himself the patient of multiple doctors, each of whom is treating, or rendering opinions on, or puzzling over, one thing and one thing only, none of whom seems to be conferring with any of the others, which not only leaves the patient feeling like Humpty Dumpty, it leaves the patient in the paradoxical position of being poked, prodded and penetrated by an endless series of experts and simultaneously feeling fundamentally unknown.

But of course it's not just medical patients who suffer that experience, and it's not just the professions that suffer specialization. The Christian life—which is, after all a profession, even if it is committed by God expressly to amateurs—has been carved up, dismembered and delegated, in pieces, to special people who have what we call "special gifts." We all know that this is what happened to the Great Commission which somewhere along the line became the exclusive responsibility of evangelists. So too charity, which we have delegated to soup kitchens and food pantries, so too the area of discipleship now called "life skills," which we've delegated to social workers, so too the corporal work of mercy called burial, which we have delegated to funeral directors. Anything the Church has failed to refer to the world it has reassigned to parachurch ministries, the professionals, save the liturgy. Safely in the hands of the clergy and professional musicians, the liturgy has become our specialty.

The practice of hospitality the Church has just about altogether forsaken. It endures in some places in the misbegotten form of house groups and potluck suppers. The problem here is not that we've assigned the responsibility to "the gifted" or the experts or the specialists—though unfortunately the practice is increasingly left to a faithful few. The real problem is that hospitality today is practiced unto a chosen few. We entertain our friends; sometimes, reaching just a little bit farther than that, we host a gathering of newcomers. These gatherings are by no means to be denigrated, except when they are advertised as hospitality. For hospitality, biblically, is not what you do for your friends. It's something you offer strangers.

Preface – by Fr. Steven Schlossberg, Rector of St. Johns Troy, New York

This book is a collection of stories about how the Church is recovering a practice too long forgotten. It's written by a man who with his wife and children discovered that practicing what the Bible teaches about hospitality changes lives. It sometimes changes the lives of the guests; it always changes the lives of the hosts. Like any other discipline of discipleship, it enlarges the life and grows the faith of the disciple who adopts it.

Much more can be said about that, and this book says it. But one thing more might be said here: when ordinary Christians like David and his family practice hospitality, they change the character of their church. My family and I went to church with David and his family for a decade, and though my family did not practice hospitality the way their family did, my family was profoundly affected by his family's experience. So were many others, many of whom probably could not account for the effect, some of whom may well have been oblivious to the effect. But the hospitality David and his family practiced infected our community and changed the disposition of our church to strangers. You may say that in practicing hospitality to internationals, David and his family were serving as evangelists. They certainly were. They evangelized our church.

There is such a thing as a gift for hospitality, just as there is a gift for evangelism. But we know that evangelization is not the exclusive purview of the evangelists, but a part of the vocation of every Christian. So too the welcoming of strangers into the Body of Christ. There are many strangers in our communities, increasingly many immigrants or foreign visitors, and the most vulnerable of these find themselves poked, prodded, penetrated and, these days more than ever, examined, tried and judged, by specialists. But they remain unknown. We know that they are known by God. This book is an encouragement, and in some ways an instruction manual, for us to help them finally know themselves as known by God.

That is the good fruit of hospitality. The beautiful paradox, of course, is that when we do that for them, we do that for ourselves. For those who welcome in the stranger become known to Christ themselves.

    Reverend Steven Schlossberg,
    Rector, St. Johns Church, Troy, New York

INTRODUCTION

Everyone's life is shaped by the places they grow up and the people they meet along the way. Growing up in various places, I always had the support of a loving family and making friends was relatively easy for me. Saying "hi" and "bye" to friends and neighbors often within the space of a year just became part of my childhood experience. Change wasn't something I feared – it was something I anticipated and expected. It meant new experiences, new friends, new neighbors and new stories.

I am grateful for the people who made a difference in my life along the way. My Puerto Rican aunt who helped me know what Spanish words NOT to use – from the word list I made at my night job as a janitor in an American pharmaceutical plant in Puerto Rico. My soccer coach and PE teacher who said to a group of us after practice one day, "Each of you will be the best Christian someone in your life will ever meet." My dad who said, "God's never in a hurry, but He's never late either." My grandmother who said, *"Kanutz, Kanutz – sufily sufily sutz!"* when my younger brothers and I got too loud or were rough housing...meaning *"Enough is enough and too much is not healthy!"* My wife who sings to my boys and me...all the time and usually doesn't even realize it. Wisdom and joy are part of my life because of the people I have and share life with.

Since 1984 I have also had the honor of meeting people from all over the world. Now I admit I have also had the privilege of traveling to several different countries for both vacation and mission work, but the people I want to tell you about didn't live far away. They were my neighbors – international neighbors who became friends. As much as my life has been shaped by family and friends from coast to coast, I have to say my life is also richer and better because of people from all over the world that have intersected my life along the way. Some were ESL students in classes I taught for local churches. Others were literally next door neighbors.

I want you to meet my neighbors. More than that, I hope you will see your neighbors for who they really are, not for the invisible people they sometimes feel like, but people I love.... and more importantly, that God loves. In the years since I graduated from a small Bible college with a desire to travel and serve God around the world, I have learned some valuable things that were not taught to me in class. One lesson is that some people from nations I wanted to visit had already come to us, and that surprised me because I had never really seen them before. I hope to share some of the gems I uncovered with you in order to help you discover the hidden blessings that are in your midst, waiting to be gathered. There are people waiting to be noticed. I must warn you, however, if you take the dare to look through a new lens at the population you live within, especially those who do not share your heritage, you will be changed.

They represent the fabric of most of our local communities. Our world is rapidly changing and becoming a smaller place. Global travel, international students, and immigration – all this means we each have the opportunity to see and actually meet people from places we many never go. I live in a relatively small city – about 55,000 people in only 5 square miles and of that number, over 15,000 are foreign born. According to the July 2015 census report 67 nationalities make up the population of our neighborhoods. We have a few colleges nearby and

Introduction

one, George Mason University, boasts to be among the most diverse universities in the US with over 125 countries represented in the student body and faculty. The nearby community college has over 180 nationalities with over 2000 international students in academic programs. It is the second largest community college in the US and according to their web site, "one of the most culturally diverse." All one needs to do is merely take a walk on any college campus in American today and look around. The world is here, studying, working, living – do we see them? Many of our local elementary schools are classified as "minority majority", meaning that more than 50% of the students are from minority groups. They beautifully reflect the diverse nature of the immigrants, refugees, international scholars and professionals that live among us. I know that for some people, these facts make them feel uncomfortable. Others, like me, get excited to be able to make friends with people who not only eat and dress differently from us but also think and pray differently. Cross cultural friendships are not necessarily easy. Language and culture shape each of us. When we meet someone whose language and behaviors are different from us, we can either build a barrier or a bridge. I chose to be a bridge builder and I hope you will also.

You see, I choose to follow the example and teachings of the greatest Bridge Builder ever. Two thousand years ago Someone was born into this world, Who in His coming, crossed an infinite bridge, of space and time, for me and for all of us. Jesus Christ came to the world to show us how to live and love – first God, and then people different from ourselves. He loved unconditionally and unapologetically. He loved when it was easy and He loved when it was hard. His love cost Him everything because He would do whatever it would take to demonstrate the depth of God's love for a broken world. I learn so much from how He spent time with people, some of them that others had no time, or interest, to meet. He cared for the foreigner as well as friends He grew up with in Nazareth and the Galilee region of ancient Israel. Life is richer today because He moved into our world to be a neighbor – to all of us. I hope you've met Him. Jesus is the best neighbor and friend one can ever have. He sticks closer than a brother, and He is always ready to listen to what we have to say – on good days and bad. It is my belief that He wants to be everyone's neighbor and friend...and so much more. He meets each of us where we are, not just geographically, but emotionally and spiritually. He meets us in our doubts and fears. He isn't turned off by our sin and shame. He meets us sometimes in our dreams and often in our friends. But He doesn't leave us where He finds us. He invites us to walk with Him, learn from Him, and He offers to carry our burdens and He shares His joy. He came so we could experience life to the full, both now and beyond.

When I look at the international people I have met the past thirty years, I have learned some things:
- All are hungry...for friendship and faith.
- Most are afraid...of rejection and misunderstanding.
- Many are hopeful...of better things than what life has given them so far.
- Each has so much to give...if we just give them the time and chance to share.

I have also learned that
- I am richer for having met people from many different cultures and countries.
- I always get more than I give when I cross cultures in friendship.
- I am humbled by the sincere faith and courage of people who come to this country with so many hopes and dreams.
- I sometimes make mistakes and have misunderstandings. But these experiences allow me to grow and learn... and at least I don't make the mistake of not loving my neighbor. Jesus tells me to do that, so I must try... and so must we all.

Introduction

In the following stories I'd like to introduce you to some of my neighbors. My hope for you as you read about some of my neighbors is that you will see your neighbors in a new way. Not all are like us...and not all like us. It doesn't matter if you share the same language or belief system – you can still be a neighbor that makes a positive difference in someone's life. It might be an international student who would welcome the opportunity to share a meal in your home or participate in one of your family's holiday celebrations. Coming all the way to the US only to see the inside of a classroom, lab, library and mall and not see the inside of a local home is a terrible waste and loss – for all of us. It might be an immigrant you work with or live near. It might be an au pair or professional who is working for a company or their country. It might be a diplomat or a refugee – both who seek to represent the best that their country has to offer, but whose circumstances of coming to the US differ greatly. All represent wonderful stories to share and experience. Most want to learn and experience some part of the American story. As you read my stories, think about an international that is in your life that you can share a cup of coffee with or simply and sincerely say a warm "hello" to. It can lead to new lessons and blessings in your life that you can pass onto others, even your children, so that the world can be a nicer and friendlier place for generations to come. After each story I will share a few lessons and blessings I have gleaned from that particular neighbor and the culture they represent.

All of my stories are true. In some cases I have chosen to leave off the name so as to protect my neighbor and friend. Safety and respect are important to any friendship and I hope I honor my international friends in the way I share their stories. They have honored me with their friendship and I am richer for having met them. For that I will be forever grateful.

Rev. David F. Case, Fairfax VA

All the commandments: You shall not commit adultery, you shall not kill, you shall not steal, you shall not covet, and so on, are summed up in this single command: You must love your neighbor as yourself.

Words of Jesus Christ

Chapter 1

Mr. A, from Afghanistan

He sat erect and dignified in his western style thrift store suit coat, dark shirt and tie and his Pashtun pants. Mr. A, a name that in his language means "servant of God", was unexpectedly surrounded by a group of the fiercest looking faces he had possibly ever faced and he was in a church based ESOL class full of Asian women.

In my morning intermediate class I realized I had a fight on my hands that I wasn't expecting or prepared for. The Asian women in the class wanted to kill this stately, nicely dressed gentleman with his balloon pants, not because they couldn't understand what he had said through his thickly Dari accented English, but because they had understood him, perfectly.

You see, my warm up topic for the day had to do with hopes and dreams for retirement. Most of my students were moms of teens and college age children, and one was already a grandmother. Church based and community based English programs attract people from every age and nationality as well as every religious and economic background. It was fun and interesting to hear the ladies in the class share how they longed for the day when they could travel, paint or have more time for hobbies like flower arranging or calligraphy. Mr. A sat still and quiet, as he usually did, not giving us much sense of whether he liked the class or the topic.

Though not an overly friendly or animated class member, Mr. A was always there and he always participated–usually offering a thoughtful response with a stoic look on his weathered face. After class, he was in the habit of waiting until the other class members had left and then he would approach me, offer his hand and his sincere thanks for the lesson. It was in these times I began to learn a bit of his story.

Mr. A and his wife were refugees from Afghanistan. They came to the US with their 7 children, lots of memories of a hard life lived in a country that changed radically from what it had been in the 1950's, and little else. In the 1950's Afghanistan was trying very hard to catch up to the rest of the world with libraries, schools for all, and paved roads in the cities. Kabul was where citizens and visitors alike looked and dressed in western attire. Then came the occupation of the Russian forces that took many lives and left the country littered with war widows and orphans and too many bombed out houses and tanks. Mr. A served in his country's army against the occupiers and rose through the ranks to become a general with much respect among his men and colleagues as he fought year after long year. Life went on, and after the Russian armies left real chaos broke out as the competing war lords and militias battled one another for the chance to shape their country's future. These military groups, known as mujahedeen, had been armed by the US as freedom fighters against the intruders and now the world watched as they turned these very same weapons on their own people. Beautiful cities like Kabul were turned to rubble as bombs and missiles reduced buildings and neighborhoods to dust. Women were forced to go "under the veil – or burka" and could no longer walk about safely in the streets to visit friends or shop openly without a male family member to escort them for basic protection as well as to conform to heavy handed religious duties they now were required to comply with. Under the oppressive authority of the Taliban, even music was forbidden and education for girls was limited to what they would need to know to be a wife and mom, not bad things to know, but as early as 14 or 15? And perhaps as the 2nd or 3rd wife of a much older man?

Eventually, Mr. A and his family were able to leave the land of their birth, but for what? Afghanistan, in spite of the incredible conflicts that have erupted within its borders, is a very beautiful country. It was their home and they would miss it. With the help of a refugee resettlement organization they were brought to Fairfax, VA. Fairfax is an small city of only 5 square miles, but with a diverse population of over 70 nationalities among its 55,000 neighbors. One of their problems is that Fairfax is a nearby suburb of Washington DC and one of the most expensive places in the state in which to live. It is hard for a modern American family with two incomes to support their 1.5 or 2 children here, so you can imagine how challenging it would be for a family of 9, with one parent seeking any kind of employment just to pay the monthly rent. Then you can add the limitations of having language and cultural barriers, and no driver's license.

Life here was not as bad as it was back home. Bullets weren't hitting the outer garden walls of the house and missiles weren't falling nearby at night, but this was no dream come true for them either. It was hard, lonely, and frustrating. Who wants to invite a family of 7 hungry, growing elementary and middle school age kids over for dinner?

Mr. A knew his strategy was to learn the language and culture of this area and that it was not merely a luxury for him, it was a survival tool he needed to be able to provide for his family so his children could have a bright future in this new land.

I also learned that Mr. A had left something behind he would never see again. The rest of his family could not accompany him. He had only been allowed to bring one of his wives and the other 2 wives and their children had to be left behind to the plunders and ravages of a society out of control. Without his protection and provision he did not know how they would survive. He was burdened by so much: those he left behind, those he brought with him, and the memories of war that kept him up at night. One day he shared with me that he was taking an antidepressant to help him deal with the heaviness of life. He also shared that coming to class was one of the best parts of his weekly routine. It was a peaceful and restful place and he felt renewed, somehow.

My neighbor, Mr. A, was of the Muslim faith that not only allowed polygamy but also encouraged it from its Holy Book, primarily to care for unsupported widow women and their families in times of war or natural disaster. He was a good man and father who loved his many children, here and there.

When all of the women had shared their dreams of retirement, I turned to Mr. A. He had a small smile on his face and his eyes were closed. Was he napping and dreaming? I wasn't sure so I asked him if he had any hopes and dreams for his later years. He inhaled deeply, sat up straight as a ram rod with his hands planted firmly on his knees, and announced to the class "My dream is to marry a young American blond woman who will give me lots of children." It was then that the optical daggers were thrown at him in stunned silence. What do you say? How do you respond to this kind of statement? With all the other classmates, after they shared "I want to paint pictures of my grandchildren" or "I want to raise chickens" others had chimed in with comments like "me, too" and "how nice." But Mr. A had just dropped a cultural bomb and the classmates felt like their culture was under attack (even though none of them were blond or especially young).

I decided real quickly not to ask him any follow up questions like "just exactly how old"" or "how many?" and thought it would be best to change the subject real quickly to our grammar lesson for the morning. As the class dismissed I overheard the lady members chuckling and giggling about their lone male classmate – the one they weren't sure they should like or hate, or both, because he had been honest.

As before, he came up to me after class, shook my hand and thanked me for the lesson. He said, "Most days I learn something – today I felt happy." We laughed and I suggested he not get the ladies angry like that again.

Though I have lost contact with him, I still see his wife – the one he was allowed to bring with him. The children are all through school now, and after he left his family in a very depressed state, they bordered on homelessness for several months. His wife and children made frequent visits to the homeless day shelter supported by local churches with volunteers, laundry and health services and hot meals… just to pick up some extra food. His wife continued in our evening ESOL classes and she eventually went to cosmetology school at a local adult education program. In addition to her regular job as a hair dresser, she volunteered each week on one of her days off at the same homeless shelter cutting and styling the hair of the other men and women who live in the shadows, poor in worldly goods and poor in spirit. She enjoys her American life, wears heavy makeup and dark lipstick and always calls me "brother" as she hugs me and plants a big kiss on my cheek that leaves a mark that everyone can see all around the room. I count her hugs among my rewards for walking with her family when very few around them knew them, or wanted to.

Her children are grown and finding their own way forward in the American Dream, and she delights to gives back to a ministry that cared for her. Such gratitude and optimism is seldom seen. I am blessed to see how she is blessing others who are lonely and poor at the local drop in shelter.

I don't know where Mr. A is today, but I know I carry him in my heart. I will always be grateful he was in my class, even if he caught us all by surprise that autumn day.

Are there some lessons you can learn from this story? Perhaps.

Lessons and Blessings from Mr. A's story:
- Everyone has a story to tell. They just need a chance to do so. When they get to talk something in them begins to heal and they begin to feel alive, and in Mr. A's words even "happy."

- We can't fix everyone's problems, but we can share the path with them so they won't feel so alone and sometimes that is their biggest problem.
- Life is complicated and worse. Life hurts. Sometimes smiles disguise broken hearts of deeply missed places and people they can't see anymore and can't forget. We have no idea of the difficult decisions some have made to leave home and come here.
- Most people from other places in the world live lives informed by some kind of faith and religious values and these may not be yours. They may actually be more like stories from the Bible (some kings or patriarchs that had more than one wife and many children and lived and fought for decades as a warrior) than we realize.
- Most of the refugees that are coming to the US are repeating the same pattern of my ancestors (and perhaps yours as well) when they came to these shores. It is hard and they work hard to meet the challenge and when they make it, they give back somehow with deeply felt gratitude and empathy.
- There is always more to a person than meets the eye.
  - Here, a well-respected officer and gentleman in his own country lived an ignored and lonely life. He was a leader of armies back home and had fought and won many battles against frightening warriors and weapons. Here, he was just another man trying hard to hold onto his dignity and get a good night's sleep.
  - The US might be called the Land of Opportunity, and for many good reasons, but for some it is the land of the lost and the home of the scared. We may not see it, but it is a reality for many. If it is to be any different for them, maybe we need to try and see our beloved land through their eyes and love our neighbors better.

I want you to be concerned about your next door neighbor. Do you know your next door neighbor?

Mother Teresa

CHAPTER 2

AZERBAIJANI WOMEN BUILD A NEW FUTURE FOR THEMSELVES – ONE PAINTING AND ONE PAGE AT A TIME

"I paint my dreams." This was the simple statement of K-, a talented artist who attended our church based English classes. I asked her about her dreams and how long she had painted her dreams.

K- is from Azerbaijan. She and another Ajerbaijani woman co-own a small restaurant in our town and it has become a favorite destination for our family. Back home her dreams almost got her put in prison – but here, she is free – free to dream and free to paint.

She shared that as a child she loved to paint. Her mother was an art teacher at a local school so she had access to paint supplies. It is not unusual for children to want to express themselves in creative ways but what was unusual was K's source of inspiration… her dreams…from a very young age.

As a young adult she had her paintings hung in a local gallery and one day the religious police came in. They were impressed, but not pleased with some of her work. They contacted her and told her to meet them at the gallery. One particular painting seemed to be their focus – it was of Jesus hanging on a cross. It is a stunning picture, rich with symbolism. The religious police asked her why she painted the prophet Jesus and told her that she needed to take it down or they would take her to prison. She responded, "I've read the Qur'an and I understand I cannot depict the prophet Mohammad in any way, but there is no prohibition about portraying any other prophet." She wasn't able to persuade them and they threatened again, "Take it down or go to prison." She took it down. She not only took it down, but she took it with her when she climbed over the mountains to leave her own country

So at her mother's urging she decided to flee to Turkey, and seek asylum. After much thinking and planning K- agreed that to live free – free to think, free to dream, free to paint-escaping was worth the risk. She paid smugglers to get her to the mountain region where she walked by foot over the border into Turkey. Since she was on foot she wasn't able to take much with her, but she did take her Jesus…rolled up and in a cardboard tube.

In Turkey she met a nice man and they married and they dreamed…of coming to America. After many years of hoping, planning and dreaming they came with their young son…and began a new life.

Many of K's dreams are religious in nature. She grew up in a predominately Muslim culture and in a well-educated and religiously observant family. Her dreams reflect her faith and they include pictures of Adam and Eve. She depicts them saddened by the consequences of their choice to follow the serpent rather than to follow God's instructions and enjoy the bounty provided them in the Garden of Eden. She has another of the days of Creation – showing the progression from darkness and void to beauty and vitality. One is a remarkable painting of a young mother with a baby...in her womb, looking very much like the Virgin Mary with the yet to be born Christ Child being tenderly caressed in her arms.

Yet the picture of Jesus captivates my attention, hence my choice to use it as the cover art for this book. Not just because of its message and meaning but because when I asked her to tell me about some of the symbols in the painting she couldn't. It was her painting, but it wasn't. It was His. In one of her dreams, Jesus appeared to this Muslim woman in a Muslim land and told her to paint Him...this way. She got up from her bed and began to paint and several hours later she had painted what He had asked of her...not fully understanding what was behind all she had done.

I asked K- if she would be willing to display some of her art in our church's art gallery and she happily agreed. Many of her creations were admired by fellow ESL students and teachers, church members, and community friends. At an exhibition and reception we hosted for her and another international artist in the community she told those looking at the painting, "People ask me what I am. Am I a Muslim, a Jew, a Christian? I don't know what to say – I just love Jesus."

K- has a partner in the restaurant, also a woman from Azerbaijan. I- teaches Farsi in the DC area during the day and then comes to the restaurant to work until closing time. She is also a pilgrim on a journey, though she didn't have to climb over mountains to get here. I got a call one afternoon from a friend who was at the city library. He told me a woman had just sat down at the table he was working at and he noticed that it looked like she had a copy of a Bible and was taking notes. When he asked if it was a Bible she said, "Yes." He asked what she was doing and she told her she was a teacher of her national language and that she wanted to translate this Book into her own language. To her knowledge, that had not yet been done and it was such an important and beautiful Book. He asked if she was a Christian and she said, "No. I am a Muslim, but I love Jesus." He found out that she was taking a break between her day job as a teacher and her other job at the restaurant and this was how she used it – to translate a few verses each day. He called me and relayed this story to me and told me she would be at her restaurant that evening. When he told me where she was from I shared that I had a copy of the Bible in her own language that a friend had recently brought me and I had it in the office. I would go meet her and offer it to her. When I got to the restaurant I found I- back by the cash register and bar and told her I had gotten a call from the man she had met at the library earlier that afternoon and that I had something for her, should she be interested. When I gave her the Bible in her language, she looked at it with wide open eyes, like a child who is surprised at opening a special gift and she hugged it to her breast saying, "I didn't know this was in my language. Now I can read it. I love Jesus so much!"

Both of these remarkable women are amazing – they came to the US to seek a better life for themselves and for their families. They wanted their children to be free to choose, to learn, to do, to be. But what I see in each of their stories is that they were also "chosen." For some reason, known only to God, one had a dream of Jesus, the Living Word of God, and He instructed her on how to paint Him – suspended over a broken world, dying to bring it healing and wholeness again. The other wanted to read and understand the Written Word of God – enough to try to translate it into her own language, not knowing that it had already been done for her by others who loved her people and loved Jesus also.

Many people come to the US with hopes and dreams for a better future. Some find what they are looking for – others don't. Coming to a new land, where one struggles with language and culture, is hard. And yet so many do and they make such sacrifices in the process. They leave loved ones behind. They leave careers and familiar life behind. They enter a new land, believing things can be better for them and for their children and their children's children. Some find freedom to work, to learn, to build a new life and do very well in their attempts to be part of the "American Dream." Others find much more – they find a spiritual freedom that leads to life on a whole new level. All are pilgrims on a journey – and for some Jesus becomes a fellow Pilgrim, and sometimes He does so in the most unexpected ways and places. As they discover how much He loves them, how can they do anything else but love Him back? And the dream goes on....

The last time I was in the restaurant K- asked me as I was leaving, "Can you tell me about baptism?" Her journey continues.

Lessons and Blessings:

- Everyone is so much more than meets the eye. The international restaurant owner, chef, and the waiter that serves you may be on a much more important and personal journey that what we see.
- Some of our international neighbors have spiritual experiences that remind us of Biblical times – they dream, and the dreams are messages from God; they meet people along the way that ask "Do you understand what you are reading?" as Philip asked the Ethiopian pilgrim in the Book of Acts.
- God is ever present – no mountains or other barriers, natural or manmade can keep Him from touching a life. That touch may alter that life in dramatic ways.
- Be a listener – a learner. Ask questions and then really listen to what international friends say. It might not "fit" your world view or experience, but since when does God "fit" nicely into our lives. He comes to comfort us in our distress, but nowhere in the Bible are we told we would be comfortable with Him or His ways. He and His ways challenge and change us and help us see ourselves and others in new ways – His ways.

It's very important to know the neighbor next door and the people down the street and the people in another race.

Maya Angelou

Chapter 3

Meet BK from Nepal

BK's story began when he walked into a morning ESL class, came up to me, offered his hand, and introduced himself saying, "My name is BK. Can you introduce me to Jesus?" In my work with international newcomers from all parts of the world for the past 30 years, I have gotten used to being asked questions like, "Do you have a Bible in my language I can borrow or buy?" However, BK's question was the most direct one I had ever gotten.

After class I heard his story and I told him more about the Jesus he wanted to know.

BK grew up in a low caste family in Nepal known as the "untouchables" in his community. It wasn't his fault, it was just his birthright or, more accurately, birth-curse. One day while he was at school, some visitors came and brought brightly colored picture books that told the stories of one of the world's greatest storytellers, Jesus of Nazareth. BK was eager to see these books but was harshly rebuked by the teacher and forbidden to get close enough to the display table to touch the books. He could look from a distance but couldn't touch. He was "unclean," but not because he hadn't washed before coming to school. He just was, as were his family and others living in the unfair caste system of their land. He decided then and there, as a child, that the faith of his homeland wasn't for him, and he would look until he found one that allowed all people to be equal.

He finished school and then joined the national police academy. As he went through the ranks, he was eventually selected to be part of a special group of security officers that would accompany Nepali VIPs on their travels abroad. On his first visit to the U.S., he slipped away from his group in Northern Virginia and essentially went AWOL—permanently. He found himself in a new land with strange customs and he had little to no money. BK slept behind a gas station, eating what was thrown into the dumpster and drinking from the water faucet for 3 days. On the third day, he noticed an elderly lady struggling to put gas in her car and he offered to help. She thanked him, told him he looked hungry, and said that if he wanted to come home with her she would fix him something good to eat. How could he turn that down?

The amazing part of this story is that after serving BK a nice meal, the woman got out her Bible and asked if he knew how to read English. He said he did, and she put her Bible in his hands and asked if he would read to her. He was shocked! This woman had just put her Holy Book in his "unclean hands" and as he began to read he remembered his childhood promise to look for a faith where everyone was equal. What he didn't realize at that moment is that even though the message of the Bible is free and available to all, and all are equal, the message is that "all are equally unclean." What was intended to be a meal with a helpful stranger became a remarkable friendship. This elderly woman invited this homeless foreigner to stay the night and—after he had stayed the night, eaten hot meals, and read her Holy Book to her for 9 months—she suggested he come and talk to the people at the ESL program at our church so they could tell him more about Jesus. She had taken him as far as she knew how and thought he needed more than she could offer.

I sat stunned as he related his story to me, and I did indeed answer questions he had about Jesus. I invited him to join our weekly Bible discussion class and learn more with others exploring the goodness of God. Not too long after our initial meeting he told me he wanted to be a full Christian. I asked him what he meant by that and he said he knew that full Christians get "wet." He was referring to baptism, and we had read in our study group about the Ethiopian treasurer being baptized after he read and understood the message of the Suffering Servant, the Messiah.

Before his baptism, I scheduled a time for him to meet the minister who would be baptizing him. BK loved math, as did the minister he met with that afternoon, so they hit it off well. The minister asked what BK did for a living, and BK told him he was a bartender at a nearby restaurant. The minister didn't think much of that as it was not his practice to drink alcoholic beverages, so he pressed BK and asked, "What do you intend to do after you are a baptized follower of Jesus?"

That's when BK said those innocent yet sincere words, "I'm going to make the best martinis and now I will do it to please Jesus." And he did for a while until he moved on to another state and we lost track of him. But we trust that BK's Good Shepherd, who loved him unconditionally when he was "unclean," knows where he is today. No doubt in my mind, he's helping to introduce people to his Jesus who makes the unclean clean.

Some lessons and blessing from BK's story:
- Not all cultures or faiths are fair. Some are cruel and wound people, even children, deeply.
- People with "hungry hearts" get fed—somehow, sometime, somewhere.
- Simple acts of kindness can lead to wonderful blessings.
- God may be the great lawgiver, but he loves all "law breakers" equally.
- There in no one so unclean, by any cultural or religious/moral standard, that the mercy of God cannot clean and refresh them, giving them new life, new vision, new purpose, new peace.
- There is power in the words of the Holy Book, the Bible. Read it, and find out for yourself.

"People glorify all sorts of bravery except the bravery they might show on behalf of their nearest neighbors."

George Eliot

CHAPTER 4

A CHINESE SCHOLAR WITH A HUNGRY HEART

"I wish I could be a parent in America. It would be so much easier." Those words were spoken by a visiting scholar from China as we rode home from a visit to Lancaster, PA for the Thanksgiving break. Our family and this highly successful and very intelligent researcher in China's space program had just spent the last 4 days visiting in the home of a Mennonite family, taking in the sites of the beautiful landscape of the many farms, rolling hills and valleys of this slice of the "American pie."

We are parents of 3 boys and we had just been with Mennonite and Amish friends who had anywhere from 6-12 children...and we knew "parenting wasn't easy." What could she possibly mean? She only had one son. Admittedly, by law, that is all she was allowed to have, but raising one child should be easier than raising 3 or 6 or even 12. We thought so, but we also thought we heard something else behind her statement, so we asked. "How would it be easier to raise a child here rather than in your home country?" Her answer wasn't what we expected.

Like many of her generation, she had grown up in some very hard years of recent Chinese history. Her education had been interrupted by the Cultural Revolution of the 1960's and

70's. When she was able to go back to school she had worked very hard to pass the notoriously difficult college entrance exams. In 1989 she found herself surrounded by thousands of hopeful, happy students filled with great expectations for their country – hoping for greater economic and political freedom.... in the center of Beijing–the historic Tiananmen Square. It was a freedom party for tens of thousands of the best and brightest of China's universities. However, hope turned quickly to despair in the early morning hours of June 4th when tanks and soldiers rolled into the Square and disbursed the crowd with live ammunition and much blood was shed. Friends she had gone with didn't come home. Some died, others just disappeared. It wasn't supposed to end this way.

By the time we met Dawn she had a son, 7 yrs old, the same age of our eldest son. He was bright, loved life, and had his whole future ahead of him…and he knew nothing of his mother's broken heart from that tragic day years earlier. Also, like most of her generation, she had been taught that the State was the highest and best authority in the land. To serve the State was the highest calling and the highest good. To help China succeed domestically and internationally was the calling and responsibility of her generation. She did contribute to China's success through satellite communications research and had been elevated to the prestigious level of vice dean of her elite university. Apart from political freedom, what more could she possibly want? She had a sterling reputation in her field and was known and respected the world over for her knowledge and skills. She had a smart and entrepreneurial husband whose success in business was tapping into the huge amounts of new money in China's booming economic development. They lacked for nothing. She had a son – something that was culturally and historically important for Chinese parents. But she wanted more – she was hungry for something more. She wanted a "good son."

As we drove down I-95 toward Baltimore she answered our question about what she meant by it being easier to raise a child in the US. She said, "I'm jealous of you. Both of us want our sons to grow up to be honest and good people. You have an advantage – you have God." I asked her to tell us more of what she meant by that and she said, "When I tell my son he needs to tell the truth he asks 'why?' If your sons want to know 'why,' you could just tell them there is a God Who is True and He is the highest authority and He wants them to tell the truth." She had just spent 4 days with a family over Thanksgiving that offered family prayers at the table before meals, read a Bible story and prayed together before bed. She had observed the children taking turns with chores both inside and outside the house. She noticed their respect for their parents and love for one another and she saw something in that family, living on a farm with simple ways, that was precious and new for her. Faith. Faith in a God who cared for each of them. Faith in a God Who gave them guidelines for how to treat one another and how to care for the earth and all they had. Faith in a higher power than she had ever imaged…and the power was good, truly good…and safe. She felt this believing family, and ours, had an advantage over her since when we taught our children important life values, like "telling the truth," we could appeal to a higher authority than ourselves…or the State, which in her mind couldn't be trusted. She could serve the State, and she did with all she had, but trust – never. Her experience was that the highest authority in her life wasn't good or true – it was simply in her best interest to serve it as best as she could, looking after her own interests and taking advantage of all the opportunities her and her husband's success could offer themselves and her son. But she wanted him to be "good", not just well educated and rich. She wanted to be able to offer him values that would help him in his life to want to be kind, helpful, and truthful – qualities she felt were in short supply among her country's newly rich and powerful.

We shared how God isn't only for Americans and that if she did believed in Him, He would help her raise her son to be an honorable person. We continued to chat and reminisce on the fun we had had with the new friends we had met in Lancaster and as we drove back into the busy traffic and night lights of Washington DC and Northern Virginia, we all felt like the simple life of the family we had left behind was a rare and wonderful thing not experienced by many of our friends in our busy and power hungry community.

The day after Christmas we got together with her again, this time at our house to make cookies and play games. She was in the US as a visiting scholar and China's policies didn't allow her to come with her family. She missed her husband and her son...and this was before Skype. As we worked and talked in the kitchen she told us about an event she had gone to the night before Christmas. It had been hosted by a local Chinese church and they had offered a nice meal to Chinese students and scholars, sung Christmas carols, and shared the meaning behind the celebration of Christmas. She said, "I now understand what Christmas is all about. It is when God gives His best gift to the world – His son." We affirmed her understanding of this special holiday and then she went on. She shared how she had thought about this special gift of God, not just to the world, but to her, as the speaker had stressed in his talk. And she had made a decision. She wanted to really participate in the spirit of Christmas and all the gift giving. After she left the party at the Chinese church that night she continued to think of what she had heard and she not only wanted to receive God's love gift, but she wanted to give one to Him. So she gave Him her heart. That afternoon at our home she stood in our kitchen with flour on her cheek and wearing an apron and she was beaming with her happy news. We congratulated her and celebrated with her as she talked about her experience with her new higher power – a heavenly Father. But she had a concern as well. She knew she had gotten as far as she had in her job at the university due in part to her Party affiliation and activities and she now saw a conflict. The State was no longer her highest authority. Could she continue to serve the State without question as she had done before or would things have to change?

In the next few months she opened her apartment to several other visiting scholars from China to watch movies about the Christian faith. She didn't tell them she believed; she just invited them to come and watch and talk about these new ideas. In April, just one month before she was scheduled to go back to China, she decided she wanted to become a baptized follower of Jesus. At the time it was common knowledge that the Chinese government had "eyes and ears" on its scholars in our area and it was not uncommon to have a Chinese "visitor" attend a church service, but then not stay for the entire service. We suspected we had "watchers" among us from time to time and as much as we wanted to honor her desire to be baptized, we were concerned for her safety. Since we couldn't baptize her at a regular public service, we arranged an afternoon private baptism for her. She got to invite the many friends she had met from both the Chinese church and her American Christian friends who had shared the path with her in the preceding months of her journey with Jesus.

She returned to her home and family a month later and resumed her work and research at the university. We had arranged for some Christian materials and books on marriage and parenting to be delivered to her home before she arrived – things she would never find in a local Chinese bookstore or library.

Her story goes on and things really changed, but not for the better. It was hard to go from an environment where each week she was with friends that would pray with and for her to an environment where she didn't know anyone she could talk with about her new faith. She asked God to guide her and help her to tell others about this gift she had received while in America. She talked with her husband, her son, her mother. They were interested in her stories about places she had visited and people she had met, but they were not comfortable with her new belief in God – this God Who had given her freedom from sin and shame and was teaching her how to live a true and holy life.

During her first year back she met another professor who had also studied abroad and had also made Christian friends. He, too, had become a believer in Jesus. She had found a spiritual brother…in her own academic building. They met to pray and read the Bible each week and began to invite some of the graduate students they worked with to join them. The weekly meeting outgrew the classroom they were using and it continued to grow…until it got noticed. She was asked to come to the senior Party member's office on the campus and was confronted about these activities. The officials told her that faith in God was not compatible with her role at the university and she needed to stop believing in Him. In typical Chinese fashion, that reminded her of the days of the Cultural Revolution, she was put into a room all by herself for several hours and told to write out her "self-criticism." She spent that time writing about God's love for her and how she had come to know and love Him. She also wrote about how and why her accusers should also come to believe in Him and accept His love gift, Jesus. Needless to say, her interrogators were not impressed or pleased. In the months to come she was not allowed to leave her home – she lost her prestigious position at the university – she was told that she needed to give up God, or her son would never be able to go to college when he got older. She told them she would surrender her Party membership and responsibilities, but she could not give up God. And God did not give her up either. Things gradually improved – she was invited back to the university, but as a low level instructor. She continued to meet with her believing professor friend and graduate students who had an interest in learning about God and the Bible. A couple of years later she came back to the US to present a paper on her research and she was able to visit us. She shared how her mother had come to believe in God, her weekly group of students had grown from one classroom of 40 seeking students into a network of 10 groups of 40 students and professionals each. They had become an "unofficial" church and had hired two full time pastors to help them learn the ways of God, how to have strong marriages and how to raise their children to love and follow the Truth. This group of 400 continued to grow and is now one of the largest non-registered churches in her city. They still get harassed by the government, but the government knows that some of the city's best and brightest have chosen to be part of this church, acknowledging that they serve not only China in their day to day work, but they also serve a higher power than the State, and that makes them good people and good citizens. They are not like many others in their professional circles who have become seduced by China's new wealth and have gained power at the expense of others. They refuse to play the games that many Chinese leaders play, they don't allow themselves to get corrupted through greed and power plays, they work hard, they pray for their beloved country, and China is better for it.

Our sons are grown now and they eventually met when our family visited her in China several years later. Her son and ours were learning to walk as true and honorable men. Parenting is hard no matter where you live, but it is so rewarding when you see the next generation seek to live and love as God, the Highest and Purest Power, guides. He alone gives true freedom and satisfies the cry of the hungry heart.

Lessons and Blessings:

- Having all the education, wealth, status and more that a person can achieve doesn't bring real and lasting satisfaction to a truly hungry heart.
- There are people in our lives and circle of influence who not only have hungry hearts, but some of these same people have the capacity to help other hungry hearts find nourishment for their souls. Some we befriend will

be used of God to do so much more than we can think or imagine.
- Some of our international friends will remain in the US, find jobs, settle down, and get lost in either the American dream or rat race of life in our busy cities and universities. Others will go back to their home countries and be in contact with family members and colleagues that need to discover the spiritual freedom they can share with them.
- God loves the nations and He is busy bringing people like us into the lives of people who have never had a chance to hear about Him. One of the best ways to share His love is to invite them into our homes and hearts for simple family activities, meals, family prayers, and just the ordinariness of our daily lives.
- Some who choose to follow Jesus will pay a price many of us will never be asked to pay. We need to not only share the blessings of God's love but help them understand the cost involved in making that important decision to give their lives to the Lord.
- When God reaches out to someone who needs Him, He often surrounds them with many of His children to show them His amazing grace. It often takes a whole community of believers to help one Truth seeker find their way to the Father's heart.

Asking questions, listening and learning before sharing ideas about faith allows people to share more of what is really in their heart.

The Bible tells us to love our neighbors, and also to love our enemies; probably because generally they are the same people.

G.K. Chesterton

Chapter 5

"Enough!" – That is What My Name Means

This was the humorous answer we got from a young man who lived with our family for over a year. He was South Sudanese, but had come to the US from Kartoum, the capital of the northern half of that divided country. Like many of his tribe, he was tall, lean, had tribal markings on his forehead...and he was one of the "lost boys." When he was 8 years old he and his older brother were forced to leave their home village in the southern regions of this very large African country and walk...over 800 miles to safety. War had come to their village and nothing was left of the huts and homes that used to stand...before the planes came and bombed everything. Family and friends were scattering. Some had died. Others were "missing in action." Niop and his elder brother set out with others on a long trek, looking to find a safe place to sleep that night.

As we chatted with our new housemate we asked what we have often asked of our housemates. What does your name mean? In the 25 years we have lived in Northern Virginia, we have been blessed to share our home with over 55 internationals – some for a few days, others for a few years. They have come from so many different countries and have exposed us to so many ways of growing up in this world. One was a young Libyan student who had 57 siblings, some he had never met. He was 19; his eldest brother was in his early 60's. Their father, a wealthy and powerful sheik, in his mid 80's, had multiple wives and multiple families – something permitted by his Islamic faith. Another was from Iceland. We could never pronounce her difficult last name. We have had several from China, others from Pakistan, Japan, Ghana, Ethiopia, Russia and Peru. All have made their mark on our lives as a family. We once asked our sons if they ever regretted living in a shared house and they said, "No way! It means we have always had older brothers and sisters to play with and to talk to." Some have stayed very private and hard to get to know. Others have made themselves so much "at home" that they have offered to help mow the grass, chop the wood for our wood stove, and one young couple even planted their own garden. Two couples that stayed with us had their first child while living with us – bringing us the joys of having a little baby in the house once again. We have shared meals, walked in the neighborhood, watched movies, played games – just everyday things that families do, but with the added challenge sometimes of not being able to communicate very well. Differences in language and culture are real differences and sometimes result in challenges we couldn't anticipate. Once a police officer showed up at our door saying he was responding to a domestic dispute. We didn't know what he was talking about until we discovered our Chinese fellow had called the police on our Ghanian fellow because he wouldn't give him a ride to the store. We resolved that – they both moved out. But for the most part, we have been enriched by these shared experiences with people from around the world. We have sacrificed privacy at times, been inconvenienced at other times, and wondered if it was really worth it sometimes.

When our Sudanese friend moved in we were struck silent listening to him share in quiet tones about his journey with his brother to Ethiopia. It was so overwhelmingly sad. To change the mood we asked him to tell us about his name. He smiled a shy smile and told he was the 8th child of his parents and when his mother gave birth to him, she looked in the direction of his father and said firmly, "Niop!"…meaning "enough!" and the name stuck. This young man worked hard as a security guard at night and went to school during the day – trying to complete his associate degree at the local community college. He lived so simply and yet seemed to always be so thankful. He worshipped with other Southern Sudanese at a nearby church where he found a new family with the other "lost boys". They laughed, played, worked, prayed and did life together. I don't know if we have been to do enough to help some of our international friends. The opportunities and needs are so great.

He, like many others, moved on and some we have managed to keep track of; others we do not know where they are now. But they are in our hearts and our family photo albums.

Lessons and Blessings:

- Our communities have so many people from so many different backgrounds and with so many stories.
- Many Americans live very insulated lives, even in ethnically diverse communities. We may see our new neighbors, but do we know them?
- Some have made such long and hard journeys, just to find a safe place to sleep at night. Others have come with so much hope for a new beginning and they need friends. Some feel "invisible" as it seems like no one wants to talk with them or hear their stories.
- Many have so much to offer – their energy, optimism, hope for what their academic studies will bring them as they learn things some of us will never be able to comprehend.
- If we would see the world, our world, through eyes that noticed the new neighbors, and if we would seek to get to know them, more would find their place in life and life would be happier…for them and us.

What a cruel thing war is... to fill our hearts with hatred instead of love for our neighbors.

Robert E. Lee

Chapter 6

Hamdiya—A Slave Made Free

Unexpected "walk ins" were one of the things I loved about my job. People might come for our English class program or for something else completely. Just before Christmas several years ago, a guest arrived who was in need of a bit of both, and so much more.

Hamdiya was from Ethiopia. She was but a child, barely 16, if that. She wasn't sure how old she was. The woman who brought her to the office was an Ethiopian immigrant and had been in the U.S. for many years. Our English programs were for adult learners, not children of immigrants or refugees, so I was surprised to hear that Hamdiya was the potential student, but then I learned her tragic story.

Hamdiya had about a 3rd or 4th grade level of education. She came from a part of Ethiopia that is still wild and untamed, both politically and naturally. Her companion that day asked if we could please accept her as she had tried other church and community programs only to be turned down due to Hamdiya's age. Classes had just gotten started that morning so I invited Hamdiya join one class and be our guest for the day and see if she would like to attend future classes. This would also give her companion and me time to chat further about the frightened but beautiful young girl she had brought into my office.

The woman first told me how she had met Hamdiya. She had been driving down the road just before Thanksgiving when she noticed a child sitting on the curb, all out of breath and crying. She noticed that the girl looked Ethiopian. As she pulled up beside her, she rolled down her window and spoke to her in Amharic—her native tongue —to simply say hello and to see if the girl was okay. Startled, the girl looked up, ran to the car, pulled open the door, and jumped in. The driver was shocked, but this was only the first shock in her story.

Hamdiya had just escaped a terrible life and was looking for a new one. At that moment, any person who spoke her language was a surprising impossibility. She had been locked in the home of her "owners," and she had just broken away, run as far and as fast as she could, and was totally lost in this new city. This happened in Northern Virginia, a former slave state a long time ago. Was I hearing the story of a modern day slave?

Six years earlier, Hamdiya's village had been raided by a roaming band of fighters when she was 10 years old. They arrived late in the afternoon, rounded up the villagers, shot the parents, and gathered up the children. Hamdiya had watched all this from a hiding place where her mother had put her as the Jeeps and Toyota trucks spun into the middle of the cluster of houses and huts. From her vantage point, she saw the men shoot her father, her mother, and her elder brother. They took her elder sister and several other children, killed many other neighbors, and then roared off. They couldn't have been in the small village for more than half an hour of terror.

Once the dust settled and all was quiet again. Hamdiya walked through the carnage. No one else beside her remained alive or was nearby. She went to the dead bodies of her family members and sat by their side in the increasing darkness. She didn't even cry—she couldn't. She was shocked into disbelief, scared that someone would hear her and come back for her, the only remaining resident of the village. Very early the next morning, they did. As she was sleeping by the side of her dead mother, she awoke to the terrible sound of a vehicle skidding to a stop nearby. She tried to run, but a man caught her, tied her hands and feet, and threw her in the back of the jeep.

I never heard the events between her capture and her enslavement to a wealthy family living in a large house in the Middle East. She was to be a house servant and do anything else her owner wanted her to do. She was young, attractive, and she could be trained. Her new owner also owned a home in Northern Virginia and so she made trips with the family when they came to the U.S. for his work and for shopping trips. Hamdiya, however, was never let out of the house. Back in the Middle East, her world consisted of the walled-in residential compound. All she could see was the sky and the tops of other nearby homes, all palatial in nature. But she had work to do, 7 days a week, and this was her life for the next 6 years. She picked up Arabic and a little bit of English, as these were the languages the family used when speaking to her. She thought she would never hear her own language again; much less ever see another Ethiopian person.

One particular day while the family was in Virginia, the owner was at work and his wife had gone to the nearby mall. As was their custom, if there were no other servants to watch Hamdiya, she was locked in a bathroom when the family went out. That day, she discovered the bathroom window could be opened, and it led out to a roof above the back patio. Somehow she managed to get out of the bathroom, off of the roof, and out of the gated property without being seen. It was a cold November day and she had no coat to wear, only her house clothes. She didn't know where she was or where to go—she only knew she didn't want to go back. So she ran along street after street and then, gasping for her breath, sat down on the curb, not knowing where to go or what to do. It was then that a car pulled up in front of her and she heard, for the first time in 6 years, someone speak to her in her own language: "Hello. Are you okay?"

Without a second's pause, she lunged toward the car, huddled in its warmth, and ducked down so as to not be seen by anyone passing by. What would you do if you were the driver, out on a shopping errand just before Thanksgiving, and this happened to you?

Well, the driver took her home and gradually learned more of her story. She washed her and ran her hand over the scars on her back where Hamdiya had been beaten. She clothed her with her daughter's clothes and made a bed for her. Hamdiya slept, ate, and hid in this new sanctuary, not knowing what was next, but knowing for the first time in years that she was safe.

Hamdiya came from a Muslim village and her caretaker was a Coptic Christian, but they were both from the same country and able to communicate with a shared language. This was the story I heard that day, just before Christmas. I was stunned. Sitting before me was a hero and a savior, a brave and strong woman of faith who was doing something unheard of. She had taken Hamdiya to a doctor, had met with social services and a lawyer, and had helped Hamdiya apply for asylum. She had become her legal guardian and was her angel. She took her everywhere — to the stores she had never seen before, to the park to walk and talk, and now to an English class, where she could learn a new survival tool, the English language of her new homeland.

Hamdiya came to class for the rest of the year. She was our youngest student ever, but the adult students loved and welcomed her into the class and into their lives. She had found room in our "inn" that Christmas season and she had found a new life with this stranger who had simply stopped to say hello to her when she was sitting lost and cold on the side of the road without any idea of where to go.

Lessons and blessings from our Ethiopian neighbors:
- There may be much more than you see when looking at another person.
- Evil and cruelty are a very real experience for many people we see each and every day. They may have suffered unimaginable horrors and need the healing that can only come from God and from the kindness of strangers willing to share their burdens.
- God is the fixer of mankind's harsh and cruel acts. He sees, weeps, and rescues, never forgetting the lost ones He loves. Only God could have arranged for Hamdiya's escape on the day and at the time her rescuer would be passing by on the same street where she sat, lost and afraid.
- Coming to the U.S. may not be a dream come true for some of our international neighbors.
- Connecting with a kind person can make all the difference in the world.
- Kindness may be more than saying "hello." It might change our schedules and our lives. We need to decide every day, "Is it worth it?" I believe it is.

"Do not waste time bothering whether you 'love' your neighbor; act as if you did. As soon as we do this we find one of the great secrets. When you are behaving as if you loved someone, you will presently come to love him."

C.S. Lewis

CHAPTER 7

MY JAPANESE NEIGHBORS—
THE TOYOTA TRAVELERS

When my wife, Cathy, and I got married in 1986, one of the first international couples we met at Virginia Tech were visiting professor Mitsuhiro O- and his wife Masako, from Tokyo, Japan. They were both educators of the highest rank. He was an accounting professor at a prestigious Christian heritage college in Tokyo, and she was a kindergarten teacher at a school that families competed to enroll their children in. But what I remember most about this distinguished couple falls into three categories: roads, sandwiches, and toilets.

We met weekly at their apartment to help them with English pronunciation and everyday conversation. While there, we always enjoyed snacks and interesting drinks. We came prepared to teach something new about our language and culture, but we did more eating and laughing about their most recent American adventure than covering any of the prepared materials we brought with us.

One of the American stereotypes of Japanese at the time was that they liked cameras and cars, and it would have been easy to have reduced Mitsu and Masako into two-dimensional characters- their two biggest hobbies were driving and photography.

But we quickly found that there was much more to them than that. I discovered that at least for this visiting scholar, his year in America was more like a year long vacation or sabbatical than a study or work abroad experience. Mitsu and Masako were middle aged. He had tenure at his Tokyo university, and Masako had years of early childhood teaching experience, but they didn't have children of their own. So while in America, they threw themselves fully into everything they did, both vocationally and recreationally.

Our weekly lessons consisted mostly of stories about their weekend travels. When they arrived in the U.S., they promptly bought a 1984 Toyota Corolla hatchback. They wanted something easy to drive, good on mileage, and Japanese. Masako loved to take pictures and every weekend—since this was before digital photography—she would take a roll or two of snapshots. She would have the pictures developed before our late week language and culture session so she could share their previous weekend's journey with us. Part of the humor was that the pictures she was so proud of were terrible—yet we couldn't wait to see the next week's travelogue.

You see, Mitsu and Masako had very defined roles: he always drove the car and Masako always did the cooking. Their weekend trips took them from Blacksburg, Virginia, to Nashville, Chicago, Niagara, New York City (where they always enjoyed staying in the Hotel Astoria), New Orleans, and many other places near and far. Many people visiting these cities for a mere weekend would fly, but not Mitsu and Masako. Their beloved car was the only way to go. While he drove, Masako took pictures of famous and favorite American landmarks from the passenger side window. He rarely stopped or even slowed the car down. That is why, from an artistic perspective, her pictures were terrible.

They would tell us about their travels, we would help them pronounce the names of the places they had visited, and we would look at blurry snapshots and all laugh.

My Japanese Neighbors—The Toyota Travelers

When they got ready to return to Japan, Masako's mother came to visit for several weeks. During this time they visited Canada. I'm not sure how much they saw, but they were gone for more than a weekend.

Our last meeting was one of our favorite ones. Masako and her mother had prepared a feast of beautiful small Japanese finger foods. Each time we thought we had finished and could have her join us, Mitsu would say something like "Oi!" and she would jump up and bring us another dish more exotic than the previous one. Once we had eaten more than our fill, we asked them to tell us something they enjoyed and thought they might miss about their time in the U.S. when they returned to Japan.

Mitsu immediately responded, "Roads!" This puzzled us a bit, even though he had driven hundreds of miles each weekend, so we asked what it was about "roads" that he enjoyed so much. He said simply, "The American roads are called 'freeways' and they were—free, that is." We didn't realize that many roads in Japan are toll roads, so he was overjoyed to have the chance, the time, and the free roads to do what he loved to do—drive. We so often take such a simple thing for granted, and yet it was something he would always remember and miss as he returned to his daily packed train rides to and from the university and a work schedule that left him very little free time to enjoy the open countryside.

Masako's word was "sandwiches." Once again we were dumbfounded and not prepared for this response, so we asked her to explain. She had just prepared a wonderful and exotic array of Japanese dishes for us with her mother's help. We knew she was an amazing cook, but she told us she loved sandwiches. To our query, she said that sandwiches were so nourishing, fun to eat, and easy to make. Her life was much simpler here in the U.S. Mitsu wanted to do "all things American," so while they were here they ate sandwiches on their journeys and for lunches in their own apartment. This was a great vacation for her as well.

"Toilets?" Well, that was the most enjoyable part of the mother's visit to Canada. I never did understand what was so special about the Canadian toilets, but it was enough that we all had a good laugh as we wrapped up our last session together.

The session ended with a great surprise. Mitsu told us he had enjoyed our times so much. We usually left their home happy but wondering if we were helping them gain any language or culture skills since we did more laughing and listening than serious talking or studying. He wanted us to do something for him, and this ended up being something he did for us. Cathy and I were getting along okay with our one car, but he wanted to leave his car to us—his Toyota Corolla that had travelled so many wonderful and happy miles. We were overwhelmed by this act of uncommon generosity, but how could we refuse? It was like he wanted us to take care of his pet as he was soon to leave her behind, and he didn't want to sell her to just anyone. Of course, we accepted, and we drove that Toyota Corolla many more happy miles as we moved to a new location, took a new job, and started our family. For as long as we drove that car, we laughed as we thought of the hundreds of blurry pictures that had been taken from the front passenger-side seat.

Lessons and blessings from our Japanese friends:
- Sometimes important people in their own cultural contexts just want to be normal, simple people. They want to laugh, tell stories, and share food and time.
- Values are different for Americans and people from other places. However, if we spend enough time listening and talking, we discover that we have more in common than we can imagine.
- Uncommon generosity is sometimes the way international friends say "thank you." It might be a wonderful meal or something more. Don't refuse the gift—if you do, you refuse the "gift giver."

- Reciprocity is a value better understood beyond our borders than by many of us. We need to see others as capable of giving to us as well as thinking we have something to offer them.
- Stereotypes come and go with time, but if we allow ourselves to see beyond the stereotypes we can see so much more into a person's joys, pains, and challenges.
- Mitsu and Masako made every weekend count. Their play ethic in the U.S. was as hard as their work ethic was back home, and they made the best of their time here. We are glad they did.

All the blessings we enjoy are Divine deposits, committed to our trust on this condition, that they should be dispensed for the benefit of our neighbors.

John Calvin

CHAPTER 8

MY PAKISTANI NEIGHBOR, WALTER AND HIS FUNNY HAT

It was cold for November. He was standing in the parking lot of the church where I worked and looking at the cross. He was wearing an old green army jacket and a hat I had seen only in the BBC news reports I watched each night—a light brown cloth cap like Afghan men wear. Was he friend or foe? My church and home are near Washington, D.C., and we, along with New York and Pennsylvania, had recently been attacked on September 11 by men who had taken over planes and killed everyone on board. The Taliban came to mind when I first saw him, but what was he doing here in our church parking lot? I walked over to meet him, and he suddenly broke into a wide smile. He shook my hand eagerly and bowed his head respectfully.

I asked him his name and he said it was Walter. That didn't sound like a dangerous name, and I discovered him to be both a powerful, brave, and wonderful warrior, but for a different army than I imagined. He came from Pakistan—the wild and troubled Northwest Frontier city of Peshawar. He was here with his family and they lived within a mile or so from the church. He was just out getting familiar with the neighborhood.

We chatted briefly in the cold and then he said he needed to get back to his family. I offered to give him a ride, and on the way I learned he was applying for political asylum. He had been the only Christian member of parliament in his city and had spoken out strongly and courageously for the human rights of the Christian minority. In his city, the "blasphemy law"—the breaking of which can result in long imprisonment or even death—was being used against humble Christians. He was the only person who could speak out in a public political setting to try to right the wrongs being done against innocent people in his community. In the parliament session, he spoke out without fear. He was not afraid to be known as a follower of Jesus Christ. Everyone knew it and some of his neighbors hated him for it. One day his driver and he approached his home to discover that the man who guarded the entrance gate had been shot. Soon after that, one of his sons was threatened and told he would be killed if his dad didn't stop talking about the rights of Christian people. In that place, Christians were barely tolerated. He was asking for respect and acceptance, but that could not and would not happen.

Walter was willing to die for his faith and his country, but he was not willing to see his family threatened, the lives of his employees taken, and his children at risk. So he applied to come to the U.S. as a refugee. As I left him at his apartment door, I wondered what his future would be. Thanksgiving was coming that week. I would be out of town, but this family had nowhere to go and, even if they had, they didn't have a car. Back home he had had a driver, but here he had nothing. All for the love of God and his people and for the love of his family—his wife and three young school-age children.

I went to the nearby grocery store and gathered up some groceries that I thought might be easy to prepare. I didn't know what they liked—rice for sure, but what else would this family of five want? When I got back to the apartment, Walter greeted me with what would become a traditional bear hug each time we met. He helped me in with the bags and the kids sat on the floor with wide-open eyes as his wife made tea (or chai) and some warm Pakistani flat bread with potatoes for me to enjoy. They had so little to offer, but they gave so freely. It was then, sitting on the floor with them, that I began to hear their story and fall in love with this man and his family.

Our church had a Thanksgiving Day service, so I invited them to attend. They came and then they came back on Sunday and the following Sunday and for the next 14 years they have come, hardly ever missing a Sunday even though they had moved further away from the church. His language was and is still very limited, for as soon as he was able to get a job as a gas station attendant, he devoted himself to working one or two shifts a day to support his family. He never had time for English language study. His wife had more formal education and, having worked as a nurse back home, had a much better command of the English language. The kids picked up the language as soon as they got into school.

Asylum was granted for this family and life began to change slowly. The local thrift store and other friends they met at the church got them "off the floor" in their apartment, and they continued to worship with us—the only Pakistani family in a mostly white church. The wife would always cover her head with a scarf during prayers , and some church members wondered if she were Muslim or Christian. Walter exchanged his old green U.S. army jacket for a wool sports jacket and yet he kept his cloth Afghan/Pakistani hat. Over time, as they made friends and got to be known at the church, families surrounded them and helped them shop for the kids' school supplies, get them enrolled for classes, take them to get the shots required to attend school, and so much more. It was Christian love in action...and it really did take a village to help them over the years, but in so doing, many were blessed.

We were changed by this family. Sad eyes but happy smiles met us each time we saw them. They were sad because of those they had left behind—who still faced the unfair and unjust application of laws they were not breaking. Happy smiles because they had found a place—a home and a church family that was learning to love them as they got to know them.

As this family got settled—as much as they could on a gas station attendant's salary—I saw extreme generosity and hospitality. You could never go to their home without getting a cup of chai and hot bread with wonderful spices or more. Walter's wife was a wonderful cook and could do amazing things with flour, oil and a few other spices and ingredients. Frequently, they would bring other new Pakistani asylees to church services with them. Even though Walter and his family had little to offer, they shared their home with new Pakitani Christian fleeing persecution and needing a place to rest and be refreshed while they looked for a room or apartment to rent.

On one church retreat, our family shared a cabin with Walter's family. After we had turned in for the night with our young boys, we heard Walter's family singing hymns in Urdu, their native tongue, in praise and thanks to God, their Protector and Provider.

At a following Pentecost service and on subsequent special occasions, Walter would get out his *tabla* (a set of Pakistani floor drums), sit on the platform in front of the holy table, and sing one of his recently written songs of praise and prayer to his Heavenly Father in his mother tongue.

A few years ago, the world was shocked at the bombing of a historic church in Peshawar, Pakistan. It was Walter's home church, and his sister and five other family members were badly injured or killed when the bomb exploded just as the service was getting out and the members began to share a meal together. To honor their faith and to show solidarity with our spiritual brothers and sisters, and Walter's true brother and sisters who had suffered so much, we held a service of prayer and worship at the church. Pakistani believers came from all over: Philadelphia, northern and central Virginia, and even New York City. It was an amazing service. I merely emceed, but they took care of the music—soulful and tearful songs full of faith in a good God walking with them in their pain. There were readings in Urdu, prayers, and a reception where all the good cooks got to share some great food.

Walter's kids are now grown. His daughter is in her second year of college, and his two sons are finding their way professionally. His dear wife, who worked so hard as a nurse caring mostly for elderly Americans, is now struggling with cancer. She is unable to work, so Walter works more hours at the gas station. His language is still very hard for many people to understand, but he is always at church—he refuses to take a shift that would keep him from regular worship with his family. They are continuing to walk with one another and others in a new and safe land to which they have come and which they love so much. I am humbled to be his neighbor. He shows me courage, faith, love for family, hard work, and an undying hope that things will get better for his loved ones back home in God's time and way.

Lessons and blessings from this dear Pakistani neighbor:
- Walter is only the first Pakistani believer I have met. There are many in our community. So many Pakistanis and Afghanis are in our county that the third most common language, after English and Spanish, is Urdu.
- I've been to their homes, eaten their meals, sat on their floors, and joined them at family prayers. At one home, the elderly grandma smoked her hookah (or water pipe) while we prayed and sang, filling the room with the sweet aroma of her flavored tobacco. It was not your typical church service, but it was holy, holy, holy as these dear ones who were persecuted for their love of Jesus in their own land tried to find their way forward in a new land.

- Work and education—they do both with abandon. Work for parents and education for kids.
- This family—and so many other international families who had established themselves as middle class members in their home countries—left drivers, cooks, gardeners, and careers behind to provide a safe haven for their children, even though it initially meant sleeping on blankets scattered on cold hard floors and not having a car or even being able to get one for a long time.
- In some lands, blasphemy is a death sentence. Someone can be charged for putting the holy book of Islam on the floor, or saying something critical of a local application of sharia law or an Islamic teacher. Different opinions and conversion are not tolerated and Christians are treated as second class citizens.
- Unlike Walter's family, many Pakistani Christians who come to our communities wind up losing their Christian identity and heritage. It is actually quite tragic. In Pakistan, they are required to carry an ID card that lists their faith in addition to their name and photo. Those with "Christian" on their card are discriminated against and refused jobs and educational opportunities, simply because they are followers of Jesus in a land where the majority follows the teachings of their prophet, Mohammad. Many Christians have migrated to or sought to be refugees in western countries so that their children can grow up free, having opportunities for education and employment that are not possible back home. Many of these families have been identified as "Christian" for three or more generations. Each generation has been relegated to jobs like street sweeping, knowing that their children will have the same jobs and future. Once they arrive in the US, many parents work two or three part-time jobs just to put food on the table and pay the monthly rent. Their faith suffers as they take every available shift, including Sundays and

holidays, to provide for their families. Often they don't see that their children are not only losing their heritage and cultural ways but are also becoming distant from their family faith. The kids are absorbing language and culture, including some western values that are not in line with the faith of their parents and heritage. Church and Christian teachings become part of their past, not their present or future. A family that has survived three or more generations of Christian faith under persecution might lose it in three years or less in a place with freedom. What was once a Pakistani Christian family becomes a Pakistani American family. By the time the parents see it, it is sometimes too late.

Geography has made us neighbors. History has made us friends. Economics has made us partners, and necessity has made us allies. Those whom God has so joined together, let no man put asunder.

John F. Kennedy

CHAPTER 9

"NO" AND "YES": JAPANESE AND BOLIVIAN STYLE

The answer was, "*My daughter needs to practice piano.*"
The question was, "*Would you and your children like to come to the beach with us and other American and international friends for a week?*"

Somehow I didn't understand A's answer, so I explained that there was a piano at the beach house and her daughter could bring her piano books and practice her lessons as often as she liked.

Once again, I got a vague answer that sounded like a diversion, and at the end of the brief exchange I thought that one of us was a very bad communicator. I didn't know anymore than when I asked her the first time about joining us for the beach vacation.

What I soon learned was that "piano practice" in Japanese English was actually "no" in this context. It was the first time I realized I had asked a "yes-no" question of someone who didn't have cultural permission to say "no" to me.

Americans are accustomed to direct forms of communication where "yes" means "yes" and "no" means "no" and usually no one is offended. It's true that Americans also have their own ways of speaking indirectly at times and creating diversions from topics they may not want to discuss or questions they don't want to answer. However, most of the time, when Americans are asked a simple and direct question, a simple and direct answer makes sense and is easily understood.

At another time we discovered this was not just a Japanese communication characteristic.

We were sharing a wonderful meal with friends from Bolivia. The wife worked at the World Bank and her husband, a former banker back home , worked as a finish carpenter here in the U.S., replacing and hanging cabinets in people's kitchens.

Amanda had just offered to serve us more of her wonderful food, and we said "yes" immediately. That sparked an interesting discussion about how different things were for them in the U.S. compared to life and customs back home. We learned that our "yes" to her kind offer would have been considered rude in Bolivian culture. They graciously and humorously told us that a guest would never agree to such an offer for more food at the first offer but rather should wait until the offer had been made three times before saying "yes." I thought this kind of verbal gymnastics was difficult, if not dishonest, but to their culture it was polite. In fact, they shared that the first time they were invited to an American home, the food was wonderful, but they left hungry and didn't even taste the delicious looking dessert because they didn't want to be offensive by agreeing to accept more food the first time it was offered. They learned very quickly that in the U.S. you must say "yes" to any offers for more at the table or the host will actually believe your "no" and take the food away. At first it was hard to be so direct, but the benefits of more good food and desserts at future meals made it all worthwhile to cross that culturally difficult barrier of polite refusal and learning to say either "Yes, thank you" or "No, thank you" directly.

I also knew another Japanese friend named Mika, who had come to the U.S. to study English for a year before starting her career back in Japan as an accountant. One day, Mika was spending time with her host family making Christmas cookies. Maureen was her host mom—relationally, not residentially as both were participating in a friendship partner program at the university to help connect locals with international students and vice versa for friendship and conversation.

Mika and Maureen enjoyed their times together, but this particular day Maureen was talking about what Christmas meant to her and her family—the celebration of the birth of Jesus. Mika's English was amazingly good for a new arrival, but she experienced something in this conversation that she had experienced with other people when the subject of God or the Bible came up. She just couldn't get it, and she didn't know why. It was if a dense fog would enter her brain and she couldn't follow the conversation This only happened when topics of a Christian spiritual nature were addressed.

Mika trusted Maureen, knew her to be safe and loving, and also knew Maureen was trying to tell her something that had deep meaning for herself and her family. And Mika wanted to "get it." So she stopped her cookie making and told Maureen of this strange "brain fog" experience she experienced when her religious friends talked about their faith in personal terms.

Maureen hadn't encountered an experience like this before, but she was a prayerful and thoughtful woman. So she said that God wanted to shine his light into Mika's life, and someone must not want that to happen, hence the fogginess. She offered to pray that this strange fog would lift so Mika could understand whatever she wanted to understand when these topics came up. As soon as she said "Amen," Mika exclaimed, "I can see! The fog is gone—tell me about your Jesus again."

The next time I saw Mika, I asked her to tell me about her Christmas break and how her time in the U.S. was going. I asked specifically if she felt she was reaching her self-determined goals for her time here. With an expression of deep peace, she turned to me and said, "When I came to America 4 months ago, I had so many plans. Some of these plans are working out for me, but I just learned something else over Christmas. God also had a plan for my coming to America. It was to meet him."

Mika's faith grew as she asked many questions, and she even began helping to lead a Bible discussion group for other international students in the winter/spring semester. Before she went back to Japan that spring, after less than a year in the U.S., she was baptized as a follower of Jesus—the Light of the world, the Light that had chased away her "fog."

I learned from Mika that when she was just an infant, her grandmother had taken her to a local temple where prayers were offered over her by the monk. Somehow, she connected that event as a very young child to her inability to hear spiritual things until Maureen prayed that the Light of God's love would chase away the darkness and confusion on that cookie making afternoon.

I confess that was new territory for me. I believed in the spiritual world and even spiritual warfare, but until I met Mika I had never thought that early events in one's life could have such a profound effect on a person as an adult. As I met others from similar backgrounds, I came to understand that the "fog" in some people's lives is not of their own choosing. They are not intentionally rejecting the message of God; they just can't get to it from where they are. Our prayers and the time we spend listening to their stories can help us help them so they can help others from their own lands find the true light of Christ.

Mika returned to Japan and found a fellowship of like-minded returnees (students who had studied abroad and had come to faith in Jesus). This group helped her find a local church. For many years, because of her strong English language skills, she provided simultaneous English or Japanese translation each Sunday during services for the preacher and the guests who attended her church.

Lessons and blessings:

- "Talking is not communicating and listening is not hearing." This is so often true when we are talking with people from other places with different social norms for polite communication.
- Some cultures do not give permission to provide direct answers. Yes or no may be the intended answer, but it might sound very different to our ears until we understand how polite communication happens in their culture or country.
- For some of these people, it is unfair at best and wrong at worst to ask them a direct question about faith when they don't have permission to say "no." Sometimes, a Christian will ask international friends if they would like to go to a church event or service or, more directly, if they would like to ask Jesus into their life. The polite answer is "yes," while the honest answer would be "no," "not now," or even "I don't know what you are saying but since I don't want to offend you I will say 'yes'." In our communication with friends from other places, we need to learn that not all cultures are as direct as ours and that if we are not careful, we will put someone we care about into a difficult situation. When people feel trapped and uncomfortable in a relationship, they tend to remove themselves; and when this happens, it causes confusion. We may think we had a wonderful conversation with someone but then discover that they don't want to get together again. Why? Maybe they feel that they were not allowed to be honest with us and don't want to mislead us.
- Understanding is more than cognitive comprehension. Sometimes, something otherworldly may be going on. As much as we want friends from other places to feel safe and welcome in our friendship and in the love of

God, there is a spiritual reality. God has an Enemy who wants to keep people away from a relationship with Him. and he is quite creative in setting up barriers to understanding in these situations.
- Although people have plans, God also has plans. Mika wanted to improve her English language skills, but God wanted her to be His child. Why did she come to the U.S.? She stated, "My purpose in coming to America was small. God's plan for my coming to America was big. It was so I could meet Him and could then take Him back to my family and friends who hadn't heard of Him before."
- We should never underestimate the value of time spent with friends from abroad, even if it is just for a fun event like making Christmas cookies. Bigger and better things may be happening at the same time.

Next to the Blessed Sacrament itself, your neighbor is the holiest object presented to your senses.

C.S. Lewis

CHAPTER 10

WHAT IS BETTER THAN "TURKISH DELIGHT?".... MORE TURKISH "DELIGHTS"

The country and people of Turkey have always fascinated me. When my eldest son was seven years old he and I visited friends in Ankara that we had met when they were in the US as visiting scholars at the local university. I was puzzled by the varieties of Turkish people, customs and expressions of faith and values – and how some cities were much more traditional or religious than others. Faith is important to me and though I would never enter a relationship for the singular reason to have a "faith talk," I do hope to explore and enjoy discussing this topic with friends regardless of their heritage or personal beliefs. This section will tell the story of 4 Turks we have met over the years. It will demonstrate some of the differences I have encountered in this complex and historic land and her wonderful people.

The first Turkish man I met was a visiting scholar at our local university and Dr. E's sabbatical year included rewriting a book on mediation and reconciliation. He was a scholar in the Institute of Conflict Analysis and Resolution. He attended our church based ESOL classes, as many visiting scholars have done – not because they don't speak, read, write or understand English – but for the very reason that they do. English is studied all over the world but the most common language spoken in the world, is not Chinese or Hindu where these nation's populations are over 1 billion people. The most common language in the world is "broken English", according to a Chinese man I heard speak at a conference. He had studied the language for years, could lecture in his area of expertise and could get papers published in world class academic journals, but....he couldn't carry on a simple conversation with a native English speaker. He lacked both the confidence and the skills to engage in casual back and forth chatting with a local person, missing some of the regional slang expressions, idioms, or the cultural framework of certain phrases which he knew were part of the language but that had not been part of his formal education in English. So he came to class with immigrants, refugees, au pairs, and other language learners…where everyone had a seat at the table, regardless of education or economic levels. His PhD meant nothing to anyone at the table because they all wanted to know how to engage in "meaningful small talk" with a neighbor, a medical doctor, teacher of their children at school or even just a gas station or 7-11 employee. Ordering a meal at a fast food restaurant was a frightening experience for some of them

As we got to know Dr. E it became apparent to him that his book on reconciliation was missing something very important…a person who could be the primary and perfect reconciler. He understood the conflicts in the Middle East and within his own homeland, the divisions and obstacles that kept communities from living together peacefully – for centuries. He had invested much of his time to both understand and try to mediate conflicts between people that had historic arguments … some so historic that the reason for the conflict was lost. Only the hatred remained. As he heard about the world view of those of us who believed that Jesus Christ, the promised Messiah, was called the Prince of Peace 700 years before His birth, he wanted to learn more. He had a typically high regard for Jesus (Isa) as any knowledgeable Muslim would, but he knew nothing of the work of reconciliation Jesus came to do or the unfinished task He left behind for His disciples. As we explored what the Bible said about reconciliation, our discussion and studies took us to the Book of Romans, written by a man who had once been a religiously motivated terrorist and torturer of those who defected from his nation's ancestral faith to follow the Way of Jesus. Dr. E was fascinated that someone like Paul could undergo such a radical life change and then spend his life commending that same inner change he had experienced to people he had nothing in common with. He was equally fascinated that the Bible contradicted some of the teachings of his own faith found in the Qur'an. Jesus told His followers to "love your enemies" not to carry out extreme acts of revenge (jihad or holy war) on those that harm or threaten you or your way of life and faith. What kind of peace maker was this man, Jesus?

Dr. E, to my knowledge, never came to know the person of Jesus, but he became a student of His amazing teachings and a fan of Paul the proclaimer of divine peace to all people regardless of race, gender, economic status or any other human measurement or divider. He and his wife returned to Izmir, the modern Turkish city so near the ancient city of Ephesus, where Paul also wrote another letter to declare the freedom and forgiveness God intends for those who will simply seek His way, and not their own.

Professor A-, on the other hand, came from the capital city of Ankara, and he came to play. In fact his favorite past time while in our city was Chuckie Cheese – an arcade game oriented pizza place for families and children. He was a nationally known lecturer and political thinker. At one point life got so full of conflict for him in his homeland that he was exiled…for thinking and speaking against the political powers with regard to freedom of conscience and religious expression. So A- and his wife, S- and their two sons came to our fair city for a year of much needed vacation and sabbatical. Their boys and ours were very close to the same age and they had a pool in their apartment complex near the campus and we didn't, so the boys spent lots of time swimming and playing together. S- taught my wife how to make baklava and I talked with A- about his hopes and dreams for his beloved country…the place that didn't really want him. I could also speak of the other visiting scholars from Turkey we grew to love and respect as they sought to bring honest dialogue to difficult issues in their land – the one who considered running for national office as president, but for the sake of his family decided to give up a political career to be a dad to his twin sons; or the judge who always had a moral question when we met – "what does your Bible say about….?" There are lots of memories of interesting conversations…but as far as I know they never led to any significant spiritual decisions but I have to believe "seeds" were sown in their hearts.

But let me now share about two Turkish sisters that changed our lives forever.

Elder E and Younger E came from Istanbul and grew up in a family that was barely religious. To "rebel" as a teenager, the elder sister wore a head covering and fasted during Ramadan, something her more liberal minded mother didn't do.

Both sisters had completed college in Turkey and had come to the US to be au pairs. This kind of work gave them the chance to improve their spoken English by living in English speaking homes and gain a new view of the world outside of their home country. Younger E came to our English class, registered, bought the book and didn't come back again until the last class at the end of the fall session. She was not a model student, but she was open and observant to "outside communications." She had dreams – not your "everyday dreams," but dreams every night… that actually came true–the next day. They were prophecies of little events that would occur, people she would meet, and conversations she would have. She would share these experiences with Elder E and together they would wonder if this was some kind of a sign from Someone from beyond. At one point these dreams began to include churches, crosses, and became more intensely religious in nature and for a totally non-religious young woman this was both curious and troubling. Jesus also appeared in some of these dreams–a name she vaguely knew but a person she was completely ignorant of. Elder E came with Younger E to the final class of the semester and she noticed a small booklet we had left for our students to pick up called "Who is Jesus?" Maybe this would help answer her sister's questions as to the nature of this strange nighttime Visitor. A few weeks later, E and E came to a meeting held at the church to help people understand the message of the Bible. The topic that night was "How does God speak to people?" One of the ways suggested by the speaker was that sometimes God might chose to speak in a dream, or other times He might speak through circumstances and events in our lives, but He always spoke most accurately and clearly through His Word, the Bible. After the lecture, Elder E came up to me and said, "E believes – now what's next?" I wanted to clarify what she meant by this so we went to a side room and I began to hear Younger E's story of her dreams and more. After Jesus began to show up she looked Jesus up online with her computer and began to read His story, the Gospels, from a website that had a Turkish version of the Bible. One night as they were together Younger E was sitting on the floor reading from Luke's Gospel about the prophecy given to Zechariah that he would have a son in his old age and he would call him John. As she read this story it all seemed to make sense and she proclaimed out loud to her sister, "It is all true! I believe this Book and I believe in Jesus." This was not good news for Elder E as she was concerned that her sister was confused so she questioned her about what might be true. Younger E didn't know how to answer that question so they agreed to learn more and decided to come to the special meeting at the church. It seemed to confirm her experiences – God had been speaking to her in her dreams and while she had been reading the Bible. So we began a discussion about what might be "next" for her, and one obvious answer was to learn more about Jesus. I told Elder E to come to the office the next Tuesday and I would give her some Turkish language materials she could take to her believing sister. She came to pick them up but had decided NOT to give them to Younger E UNTIL she had read them herself. One week later, she came back to the office, this time with tears in her eyes and she said, "I believe, too. Now what's next?" I asked how she came to believe and she held up the Injil (New Testament) I had given to her the previous week to pass onto her sister. She had read the whole New Testament in one week and when I doubted her, she took out a notebook with page after page of questions that a Muslim woman might have – "I didn't know Jesus fasted. Do His followers fast today? What does this passage (in I Corinthians) mean about women's hair and head coverings? How come women can't speak in a church?" I was absolutely amazed at her knowledge of what she had read, her humble heart to try to understand and desire to follow this new revelation of God to her. Within two weeks both Younger E and Elder E had passed from darkness to light …and we would soon see what "next" would mean for each of them. Their stories are still unfolding, their family is still trying to understand why Jesus makes them happy, both are married now to men who love and follow Jesus and who aren't Turkish. Both became avid Facebook evangelists to all their friends – they took down some of their party pictures (they hadn't been very conservative Muslims) and replaced them with Scripture texts and songs of hope and faith in Turkish. They were baptized together a year and a half later and both have found ways to serve and lead in their local church's ministries – one now living in the US and the other back in Turkey. They read the Bible voraciously and any other book we could loan or give them about matters of faith. What has followed is a life fully devoted to following this Jesus who showed up in Younger E's dreams. In one dream in particular, Jesus told her she would not make this journey alone…her sister, Elder E would soon join her. And that is what happened and today these sisters are bright lights to their Turkish family and friends.

Some lessons and blessings from these delightful Turkish neighbors:

- God, in His providence, brings some of the most amazing people into our communities, and if we are willing, into our lives.
- Not everyone we want to share our faith with wants to hear, and then some are hungrier that we could ever imagine.
- Turkey is a land of many contrasts – don't assume that when you've met one Turk you've met them all. We can't say that about our country either, or any country for that matter. No matter how much we want to "simplify", we can't and shouldn't. We need to assume the posture of a listener, learner and friend – not comparing one person from one location to anyone else we may have met from that same place.
- Many people are asking the right questions, "How can people live in peace?" and sometimes we can direct them to the Prince of Peace, where they will find the answers to their heart's questions.
- God moves in very mysterious ways to show His love… and He is more creative that we often give Him credit for. He is the primary seeker – and finder – of those who seek for Truth with hungry hearts.
- We are made for eternity, but we must live in the moment….moment by moment. Ours is to love, learn, pray and play and watch God bless both us and others in simple and sometimes confusing relationships.

Epilogue

I have told you about some of my neighbors. Who are yours? What stories can you tell about the people that have shared your life? Lessons and blessings are around every corner, especially when we are willing to make the turn. I hope in your journey you will turn toward someone from somewhere else – an international newcomer. Here are some "TIPS" that might help you in your friendships with people from the places I have written about. Whole books are written about these countries and cultures and if you have a friend or neighbor from some other place, you might want to read some of those books. Learn what you can. But in the next couple of pages I want to summarize some of my observations on the cultures I have mentioned. My comments might sound stereotypical and over generalized, and some of them are, but one has to start somewhere. So I begin with the "general" and will let you find the "specifics" about your international friends. They all have a story to tell and a culture that has shaped them. Watch, listen, learn.

Bolivia – Latin Culture
- Many Latin American countries, starting with Mexico and heading south to include Central America, South America, and some – but not all–of the Caribbean Islands, speak Spanish.

- A common language does not equal a common culture. For example, America and England – two countries "separated by a common language" are very different places. Countries with a shared language will often share a common history and that will affect values and beliefs but that doesn't make them the same. Similar doesn't mean equal.
- Latin American countries have been profoundly affected by recent past and on-going social turmoil. Crime, conflicts, political corruption, scandals and civil wars have interrupted the education for many Latin American adults and some of our Spanish "speaking" neighbors are not Spanish "reading" neighbors. Illiteracy is common with some from Latin American cultures for adults who grew up in the 70's, 80's and early 90's. Also, communities that are heavily influenced by the illegal drug industry have been very negatively impacted. Fear and mistrust is common and life is valued because they have seen life senselessly lost to gang and mob violence, kidnappings, and extortion.
- One reason so many "Spanish speakers" are living in North America today is due to violence, and lack of economic opportunity (jobs) in their own country. Coming to the US, even illegally, can appear to offer a better livelihood than trying to stay in a city or neighborhood that is wracked with violent crime, corrupt police officers and politicians, and little opportunity for children to grow up safely.
- Most Spanish speaking neighbors have been deeply influenced by the Roman Catholic Church. They may believe in God and Mary the Blessed Virgin, and respect the Bible (though few have read it). Religious devotion tends to be more a "woman's thing." For many, even devout Catholics, their faith may be uninformed due to lack of regular church attendance and even if they

attend church regularly there may be little to no opportunity for discussing and asking questions about the Bible's message.
- Pentecostal and Protestant churches are in the minority in these Catholic majority nations, but their increasing numbers and the vitality of their faith have influenced many of our Spanish speaking neighbors.
- There is a lot of wealth in Latin American countries, but much of the new money is not the result of honest work and the gap between rich and poor is getting wider and wider.
- Families are important in Latin American cultures. Food, festivals, and lively music all help these cultures feel "warm" or even "hot." Hugs, kisses, laughter are enjoyed and shared freely.
- Manners are ingrained in children – respect for an authority figure whether they be the parents, grandparents, church leaders, teachers, and employers is very common.
- We find many well educated and wealthy Latin Americans living in our communities. One reason they have left their beautiful homes and families is because careers often end when a worker, even a professionally trained engineer, reaches the age of 50 or 55. Companies can pay less money to younger workers and due to high birth rates; there are a lot of young people seeking their place in the job market. Some come to the US legally to be a tourist or visit family members, but then they decide to stay. Working illegally in the US, even at a lower paying job than their education and training would command if they had legal documents, is often preferred to being middle aged, unemployed and trying to provide for and educate children back home.

- "Latino", "Hispanic" – we hear and use these terms almost interchangeably. Ask your Spanish speaking friend what term they think accurately describes them and why.
- Since European conquest and colonialization is part of their national history, many Spanish speaking adults actually have more recent European ancestry. Before and during World War II, many Jewish families migrated to South America to escape persecution from the Nazis. After the war, many Germans and others seeking a new life came to South American countries.

Afghanistan (and other countries with refugees affected by war)
- War displaces people. Refugees flee fighting and often seek safety in a neighboring country. In many cases they are unable to go back to their homes and families and they face the difficult decision: do I stay here in the refugee camp, try to assimilate into the host culture, or seek the help of the UN to migrate to a new land. UNHCR handles thousands of requests for people seeking asylum for religious or political safety and many of those thousands end up in our neighborhoods. I don't understand why Somalis end up in Minneapolis instead of Arizona where the climate might be more familiar to them than harsh winter snows and cold. I am puzzled by the huge numbers of refugees settled in the greater Washington DC, Northern VA area. It is such an expensive area to live – housing costs are higher than most other places in America…and the new refugee gets little sustained support to help with their transition.
- The refugees I have met are of many faiths and come from many lands. Some are traumatized by not only the circumstances that forced them to leave their homes, but they are also overwhelmed by what they face when they get here. Needs for housing, furniture, jobs, transportation, schooling for their children and friends. Social

Epilogue

workers can help in so many ways, but they are often dealing with huge caseloads so many needs go unmet.
- Some refugees struggle with both English language and cultural challenges in addition to low income and limited job prospects. Some are highly educated and led successful lives back home – where they were respected and honored. Here they are fortunate if they get a clean place to live and a part time job…or two… or three, just to make ends meet.
- While fear, trauma, depression and ignorance of our social rules and customs may plague many refugees, most have a strong work ethic, are courageous survivors, and have so much to offer. Don't underestimate the ability and desire of an international friend, in humble circumstances, to bless you with the best they can offer. Many come from cultures where the US might be considered by some to be the "enemy." But many are here because they supported the US efforts to help their country as a translator or cultural liaison. These are brave people, generous with the little they might have, and love to talk with new friends.

Sudan and Ethiopia – Sub-Saharan Africa
- I've told two stories of African neighbors – one of a Muslim young woman and one of a Christian young man. Their countries are different, even though both are sub-Saharan countries. Africa is very complex politically and religiously. In these days, it looks as things will only become more so with the emergence of a more extreme version of Islam mobilizing forces against both Christians and against Muslims that it considers to not be devoted enough. Both fall into the same category as "infidels" and face tragic treatment.
- Africa is a land of so many various cultures, languages and political systems that we in the West need

to understand that "Africa" is not uniform. Many who come to the US are seeking asylum for religious or political reasons. Many more take advantage of the US Green Card Lottery system. For those who gain entrance to the US via the Green Card Lottery system, at first they celebrate a "dream come true." Some are able to gain traction as they settle in communities with ethnic subculture support. Others find that limitations with language and job skills, combined with the expectations of family members back home that they will "make it rich" in the Land of Opportunity, make the "dream" become a "nightmare."Books have been written about Africans and money and they are worth reading, but my experience with my African friends is that many are skillful survivors. Though I don't think I have actually been fully "lied to" when talking with an African friend facing a financial crisis, my experience is that sometimes they didn't tell me the whole truth. As I got invested on helping them solve a financial problem and began to check my network of fellow caring people, ministries, social support systems for resources I discovered that they had also been contacted by the same person…who had failed to tell me of the ways they had already sought assistance and had been helped.Some of my African friends adapt better than others to the "American way" of life. All inspire me with their courage and hope that things will get better if they only keep on working, networking, and praying. They have a love for music, dance, and laughter. Many of my African friends are great story tellers and time is not a big concern to them. Be prepared to spend lengthy periods of time in good company.

- Those from Christian backgrounds may have had leadership roles in their home churches and are eager to find ways to serve in local churches here. There are both ethnic and language based churches in communities where there is a concentration of people from that language group – even denominational churches that reflect some of the missionary efforts of the last two centuries to bring the Christian faith and teachings to their ancestors. However, African traditions, colorful clothing, and culture tend to accompany and flavor their Christian faith. I recall a funeral service for the brother of a friend from Ghana. Because he had been a prince in his village, there were interesting ways to honor him with rituals unfamiliar to me as a western Christian. At this unique memorial service and as one of the few white people it was my time to watch, listen, be both confused and yet impressed with how they honored the passing of this loved one.

- In some respects, those who have adopted western liturgy based denominations (Anglican, Methodist as only two examples) hold onto traditional ceremonies that reflects a very formalized expression of Christian faith that seems "old fashioned" to many contemporary American Christians. Their services here may tend to hold a strong resemblance to the more formal protocol taught them by our European and American ancestors who ventured into their lands and villages with a strong emphasis on teaching a western or denominational expression of the Christian faith rather than to allow it to become nationalized or enculturated. Sometimes custom and creed are held with the same degree of loyalty. Of course we can see the same in some western churches where denominational loyalty remains firmly rooted to the culture of the church even if the fervency of personal faith has been replaced with devotion to an agenda of social change and accomodation. For many of our African friends, they hold the essentials of their faith firmly and often struggle with the more liberal or "progressive" views of their American denominational brothers and sisters.

- I can't speak extensively about those from Islamic faith traditions, but you will see those who hold to the more conservative customs of how to dress, women who are covered, and then you have those who work very hard to be accepted by the Westernized culture. It is a time of culture crisis for many as they seek to raise their children bi-culturally – wanting them to respect their national heritage and yet trying to let their children adapt to some of the social norms of the west. This is true for most immigrant parents–How much of the Western culture of ok? And how much of national culture is non-negotiable and must be maintained? These are issues European immigrants faced a couple of generations ago and as we can see, loyalty to heritage fades with each successive generation. It makes for family tension and division.
- I have found my role as a friend of those trying to raise their children bi-culturally is to encourage the young generation to look for ways to honor and respect the values of their parents and to use discernment in how much of modern American culture to accept. Just because it is popular doesn't make it right or safe. For the parents, I have encouraged them to let their love for their children be expansive – realizing their children are not growing up in the confines of cultural restrictions back home, and they will adapt naturally to new norms. They came to the US to raise their children – now they need to allow their children to find their own place in this new land and culture, even if it is not always according to the old ways.

China, Korea and Japan – Eastern Asia:
- Names have meanings. Ask your East Asia friends who named them and what their names mean. This can be a fun and enjoyable conversation to get a glimpse into an important cultural difference. It helps if you also know

Epilogue

the story behind your own name and what meaning it carries.
- "All Asians look alike" – to some of us that is. But if our Asian friends would be honest enough to express how they see Americans, some of them would say "All Americans look alike" – at least those of European ancestry. But skin deep similarities don't unite all of us or all of those from Asian countries. We need to recognize that there are many differences between East Asia, South Asia, South East Asia and even the Middle East which is more Asian than European or Western in its culture and conservative values.
- Eastern Asian countries – China, Japan, Korea and other Pacific Rim countries have rapidly recovered from the devastation of the wars they have lived through in the last century. Economically they have become giants in manufacturing, high-tech communication, transportation and trade but often at great cost to the family system that once defined their history and values.
- The largest number of international scholars and students in the US, for several years, have been from China, India and Korea. Now, tens of thousands of Saudis, and those from Dubai and United Arab Emirates populate our university campuses of all sizes and types.
- Most of these scholars have spent years studying English and may have a grammatical advantage on the native American English speaker. But listening and speaking skills are lacking as that has not been emphasized in their own country based language training. They are often eager to speak English, but need to be encouraged that it is better to speak and make mistakes than to not speak at all. "Face saving" is a deeply engrained cultural trait and they not only don't want to be embarrassed, they also don't want to embarrass someone they respect.

- Communication styles differ – Western culture stresses clear and direct "yes" "no" answers. Eastern culture doesn't often give cultural permission to say "no." We need to let our East Asian friends know that saying "no" to us is not only allowed, but is it important if we are to understand each other. It is not rude to decline an invitation. It is ruder to just not show up or follow through with something when they said they would.
- Education is "king" – for most educated East Asians. Before coming to the US, they have devoted almost all of their time to academic studies. Family honor is very important and one way to honor parents is to excel in academics. Entrance into their high level national schools is a great honor and requires extreme effort. Entrance into a prestigious US school also shows hard work, but also it may show good connections, and money. Nonetheless, don't make the mistake of assuming that because someone is Asian, they're necessarily "good" at math or science- stereotypes, even ones that seem positive, are always dehumanizing.
- Asians may seem to be "polite" to Americans due to the different ways we communicate with one another and within our own groups. Some Asian languages (Korean for example) have formal and casual ways to talk with people who represent a difference in age, status or other social standing.

Regardless of where our new neighbors are from, they want and need to find American friends. This is often a puzzle for them as they experience an initial friendliness and politeness with many Americans, but then the relationship doesn't progress as they hope. I have heard friendship with Americans described as "a mile wide and an inch deep." The fault lies with both the international and the American. They have expectations that reflect their understanding of friendship from their home country and culture – usually homogenous in its makeup. For many, relationships with others are more important than personal time and space. For many Western Americans, we are comfortable with being kind on the surface, but we may not have room in our life for the kind of friendship desired or needed by our international neighbor. We do value time and personal privacy as a culture and though we are often generous, we share it usually on our terms – within the bounds of our own comfort zone.

In order for friendship between cultures to happen and grow, both need to adjust. We need to step beyond surface friendliness and want to both invest in and be willing to accept the offers of our international neighbor. If we assist someone from another culture, especially a culture where reciprocity is an important relational equalizer between parties, we need to accept their offers of appreciation. To give and not allow them to also give of themselves, according to their cultural ways (a meal, a gift, etc…) is to create an unfair, unequal and unsustainable relationship. Give and take we understand. We just need to put it into practice and never underestimate the ability of international friends to show kindness to us regardless of their economic or cultural ability.

Jesus, the Great Bridge Builder, shows us how to love the stranger and make friends with our international neighbors. He listened, spent time, spoke truth lovingly, gave sacrificially, defended the weak, worked for justice, and accepted the gifts of His friends. He allowed His feet to be washed by a woman that wanted to give Him her thanks and love. He accepted and blessed the gift of a little boy so that it fed many who came to hear Him teach. He met with people at odd times, like Nicodemus who came to Him under the cover of night. He touched people who were considered untouchables, showing that He knew they were people of dignity and worth even if others didn't treat them that way. He was simply available to be a kind companion to any who came His way. He welcomed little children, ate meals with tax collectors, traveled with uneducated fishermen, healed lepers and even spoke highly of the faithful devotion of a Roman soldier. These were the people on the periphery of His culture – the ones others rejected or found hard to be friends with due to differences.

When asked "Who is my neighbor?" Jesus answered with a story of a man who was on the periphery who showed great kindness to a wounded and exploited man. This Good Samaritan who came to the rescue of the robbed and wounded traveler was a good neighbor for many reasons. He didn't let social and ethnic differences between him and the wounded man keep him from doing the right thing. What was the right thing? He stopped in his busy schedule, really looked at and saw the person in need, assessed the situation, helped as he could, found someone who could help even more, and then checked back later to see how he was doing in case he could offer more assistance. This good neighbor described by Jesus was not the one His questioner had expected. His point was that God can use anyone who is willing and available to bless and help another. Maybe you feel unqualified in some ways to meet, serve and bless a new world neighbor. But you may be the best person in their life to share the path with them for now. It may be costly – love usually is; but I predict it will also be rewarding. You will grow, see others and yourself with new eyes, and help make both their life and yours better. Many have challenges we can help with. Some have problems that we cannot solve. But the greatest gift we can give to someone who is new and alone is the gift of companionship. The journey may still be hard and the adjustment to a new life and land may still be difficult, but you can be a "culture coach" to some and a change maker for others. One thing is for certain, if you will meet your international neighbor with an open heart and mind, you will be the beneficiary of some very special memories and enriching friendships. You will never be the same; and neither will they. This world will be better because you crossed the cultural divide, bridged the ethnic gap, and shared grace and space with someone who also has so much to give.

Then, go share your own stories – the successes and the frustrations. Invite others to join you – building bridges is always better with others alongside. Someday soon, I hope you will also say to a friend or family member, "I'd like you to meet my neighbor."

Conclusion

When I look at the international people I have met the past 30 years, I have learned:

- All are hungry…for friendship and faith.
- Most are afraid…of rejection and misunderstanding.
- Many are hopeful…of better things than what life has given them so far.
- Each has so much to give…if we just give them the time and chance to share.

I have also learned that
- I am richer for having met people from many different cultures and countries.
- I always get more than I give when I cross cultures in friendship.
- I am humbled by the sincere faith and courage of people who come to this country with so many hopes and dreams.
- I sometimes make mistakes and have misunderstandings. But these experiences allow me to grow and learn… and at least I don't make the mistake of not loving my neighbor. Jesus tells me to do that, so I must try… and so must we all.

O God of love, we ask you to give us love:
love in our thinking, love in our speaking, love in our doing,
and love in the hidden places of our souls;
love of our neighbours (sic), near and far;
love of our friends, old and new;
love of those whom we find it hard to bear with us;
love of those with whom we work,
and love of those with whom we take our ease;
love in joy, love in sorrow,
love in life and love in death;
that so at length we may be worthy to dwell with you,
who are eternal Love. Amen.

Most Reverend and Right Honorable William Temple,
Archbishop of Canterbury from 1942 - 44

This ancient Celtic symbol, adapted and carried by the author, shows the Eternal Unity and Community of the Trinity of the Godhead - Father, Son, Holy Spirit.

The added letters - F, H, L for Faith, Hope and Love invites God, Who seeks a people among Whom He can dwell, to help us be the ambassadors for the Lord of Heaven and the Hope for the Nations.

The symbol of the fish reminds us that Jesus alone is the bond that holds all together for the Glory of God.

CPSIA information can be obtained at www.ICGtesting.com
Printed in the USA
BVOW08s1933240216

437972BV00001B/2/P